JOB SEARCH IN ACADEME

Communication: The Department of Communication Studies at Virtual Tech seeks applicants for four tenure-track Assistant or Associate Professors beginning August 1999. Two Public Relations Assistant/Associate Professors: Teaching and research expertise in public relations: ability to teach among principles, writing, cases, and campaigns required; related content areas such as organizational/corporate communications; fund raising; public opinion research; computer-mediated communication in public relations; or health, political, or sports/entertainment communication desirable. One Information Technologies Assistant Professor: Teaching and research expertise focusing on the history, social impact, policy and/or theory of information technologies required. Related specialization in mass media effects desirable. One Telecommunications Assistant Professor: Teaching and research expertise focusing on telecommunications management, economics, and policy required. Related content areas such as telecommunication law and/or history desirable. To be considered at the Associate Professor level, applicants must have an earned Ph.D., provide evidence of excellent teaching, and demonstrate a strong record of research or professional experience. Ph.D. preferred for applicants at the Assistant Professor Level. Applicants who are ABD will be considered. Information about the Virtual Tech "Minority Faculty Mentoring Program for ABD Fellows" is available at http://www.vt.edu: 0000/admin/provost/rasprofe/wdencem. Anticipated starting date for all positions: August 1, 1999, pending funding approval. Application letter, curriculum vitae or résumé, and names, addresses, and phone numbers of three references should

JOB SEARCH IN ACADEME

Strategic Rhetorics for Faculty Job Candidates

Dawn M. Formo and *Cheryl Reed*

FOREWORD BY *W. Ross Winterowd*

STERLING, VIRGINIA

STYLUS PUBLISHING, LLC.

COPYRIGHT © 1999 STYLUS PUBLISHING

Published by STYLUS PUBLISHING, LLC.
22883 Quicksilver Drive
Sterling, VA 20166-2012

Distributed outside North America and Latin America by:
KOGAN PAGE
120 Pentonville Road
London N1 9JN
United Kingdom

Stylus is a registered trademark of Stylus Publishing, LLC.

Library of Congress Cataloging-in-Publication Data
Formo, Dawn M. (Dawn Marie), 1968–
    Job search in academe: strategic rhetorics for faculty
    job candidates / Dawn M. Formo and Cheryl Reed;
    foreword by W. Ross Winterowd. —1st ed.
        p.   cm.
        Includes bibliographical references (p.) and index.
        ISBN 1-57992-010-x (hardcover: alk. paper). —ISBN
    1-56922-011-8 (pbk.: alk. paper)
        1. College teachers—Employment—United States.
    2. Universities and colleges—Faculty—Employment—
    United States. 3. Job hunting—United States.
    4. Employment interviewing—United States.
    I. Reed, Cheryl, 1952– . II. Title.
    LB231.72.F67   1999
    650.14'024372—dc21
                        98-41905
                          CIP

ISBN 1-57922-010-x (cloth)
ISBN 1-57922-011-8 (paper)

Printed in USA on acid free paper.

We dedicate Job Search *to the people who cheered us on: Cheryl's husband, Tony, who has heard more about our searches and our writing processes than is reasonably healthy; her sons, Colin and Samuel, on whose couch it was written; Dawn's family and friends (thanks for your good humor!); and, of course, to our future colleagues, whom we hope to tell you about in the sequel.*

CONTENTS

ACKNOWLEDGMENTS

Many thanks to our savvy, proactive, innovative contributors—some of whom will be serving on search committees as this book goes to press, and some who will be using this book to negotiate their own job searches: Roger Arnold, Bonnie Bade, Mamoun Bader, David Barsky, Greg Beatty, Staci Beavers, Virginia Carroll, Susie Lan Cassel, Dianna L. Bourke, Joy Castro, Jerome Curry, Michael Day, Christopher Devenney, Alex Durig, Regina Eisenbach, Victoria Fabry, H. Kassia Fleisher, Paula Garrett, Ranjeeta Ghiara, Ellen M. Gil-Gomez, Kathleen Godfrey, Gina Grimshaw, Laurie Grobman, Joan Hanor, Casie Hermansson, Kevin Igasaki, Mary Kay Jackman, Alan Kalish, Mark C. Long, Karen J. Lunsford, R. Tandy McConnell, Patrick Thomas McCord, Michael McDuffie, Margaret McGeachy, Toby Mintz, Moe Meyer, Bud Morris, Cherie O'Boyle, P. Kevin Parker, Robert Pesce, Sandra H. Petrulionis, Jerry Pitzl, Donna Reiss, P. Wesley Schultz, M. Angela Schwer, Patricia Seleski, Richard Serpe, Laurie Schmelzer, Lynne Stallings, Darci L. Strother, Robert D. Sturr, Marcy L. Tanter, Jacqueline Trischman, Jennifer C. Vaught, Rachel Walker, Anibal Yañez-Chávez, and Jeanne

Marie Zeck. Our hiring institutions also supported each of us with research grants: Dawn received a Faculty Center Research Grant from California State University, San Marcos, and Cheryl received a Research Development Grant from Pennsylvania State University, Hazleton.

Our thanks to the Modern Languages Association for kind permission to reprint Table 1 from the *MLA Newsletter*, Summer 1998, reproduced in the Foreword. We also gratefully acknowledge the permission of Bedford/St.Martin's Press to reprint the figure on page 42, reproduced from *The St. Martin's Guide to Teaching Writing*, 3rd edition, by Robert Connors and Cheryl Glenn.

FOREWORD

W. Ross Winterowd

Particularly in the humanities, but also in chemistry, mathematics, and other scientific and social-scientific fields, the job market for new Ph.D's runs from unpromising to grim.

An article in the November 1994 issue of *Science* reported that academic appointments of Ph.D-level scientists had been declining for over two decades (*Final Report*, 16). In the academy, as in industries such as retail merchandising and fast foods, part-time employment is becoming more and more prevalent since institutions have minimal obligations to their part-time employees, who normally do not qualify for health care, pensions, and other costly fringe benefits. Part-timers in the humanities, particularly English, are appropriately called "freeway flyers," eking out a living by teaching one class here and another there. The data in Table 1 below are worth pondering (*MLA Newsletter*, 2). Fewer than half of the job-seekers in the five disciplines secured tenure-track positions. However, only a relatively small percentage had no employment. In English, for instance, 33.7 percent found non-tenure track positions, either full-time or part-time. Interestingly, 12.6 percent were employed outside the academy. In other words, there *are* jobs for those who have the will and the ways to find them. (In English, according to the *MLA Newsletter* of

TABLE I

PH.D PLACEMENT IN 1996–97, BY FIELD AND TYPE OF PLACEMENT (NUMBERS AND PERCENTAGES)

	Tenure-Track Appointment (Percentage)	Full–Time Non Tenure-Track Appointment (Percentage)	Part-Time Non-Tenure-Track Appointment (Percentage)	Postdoctoral Fellowship (Percentage)	Academic Administration (Percentage)	Employed outside the Academy (Percentage)	Not Employed (Percentage)	Total Ph.D.s with Known Employment Status* Number	Percentage*
English	373 (33.7)	281 (25.4)	147 (13.3)	38 (3.4)	31 (2.8)	139 (12.6)	97 (8.8)	1,106	93.5 (1,183)
Foreign languages	254 (40.6)	167 (26.7)	55 (8.8)	11 (1.8)	7 (1.1)	76 (12.1)	56 (8.9)	626	94.1 (665)
Comparative literature	41 (43.2)	18 (19.0)	8 (8.4)	6 (6.3)	3 (3.2)	5 (5.3)	14 (14.7)	95	91.4 (104)
Linguistics	40 (28.4)	34 (24.1)	13 (9.2)	15 (10.6)	0 (0.0)	25 (17.7)	14 (9.9)	141	81.0 (174)
Classics	16 (30.8)	18 (34.6)	3 (5.8)	3 (5.8)	1 (1.9)	4 (7.7)	7 (13.5)	52	98.1 (53)

*The percentages in this column indicate the proportion of all doctorate recipients covered in the census whose employment status is known. The numbers in parentheses indicate the totals on which the percentages in this column are based; these totals include Ph.D.'s whose employment status is known and those whose status is unknown. Other percentages in the table (in parentheses) are based on the number of Ph.D.'s whose employment status is known.

Source: MLA Newsletter, Summer 1998. Reprinted by permission of the Modern Language Association.

Summer 1998, only 8.8 percent of job seekers failed to find any employment—related, I presume, to their academic training. One hopes that the 12.6 percent who found employment outside the academy are now well-paid staff persons at foundations and up-and-coming executives with industries. On the other hand, in regard to those who found no employment within the scope of the MLA study, one has visions of the legendary Ph.D cab driver.)

Paradoxically, the goals and values of the scholarly world are in conflict with the goals and skills needed to secure a job in the academy. The goal of scholarship—at least in theory and in the shibboleths of the academic fields—is the disinterested advancement of knowledge, a selfless quest for at least a provisional truth; the values of the scholarly world often devalue the practical in favor of the ideal. The goal of the job seeker is to secure a position that will provide a living salary, and the skills needed to accomplish this goal are for the most part practical. I almost hesitate to say what I think to be the obvious truth, for in terms of academic idealism, my statement seems utterly crass, philistinic: The job seeker needs to *sell* him- or herself to a prospective employer. This effort involves good *public relations*, conveying the right image, putting the most favorable spin on one's applications.

For any confirmed academic (such as myself), those terms are odious: *sell, public relations, image, spin*. They connote ad agencies, political consultants, and used car salespeople. A more appropriate term, of course, is *rhetoric*, and *Job Search in Academe* is a book about the *rhetoric* of finding a position in the academy. As Kenneth Burke has said, and as all sensible people know, to convince people, you must speak their "language," identifying your ways with theirs (55–59). This attempt to *identify* with others is hardly mendacious; in fact, it is at the very heart of human relations (if they are amicable and productive). Identification entails such profound issues as one's ethical and intellectual commitments; it entails such apparently trivial matters as the way one dresses.

Thus, I would reformulate the concept of job search from selling oneself to *identifying with prospective employers*. As Formo and Reed make clear, identification is not always desirable or even possible—for instance, when an applicant must falsify his own scholarly and ethical values in order to be considered for a position or when the applicant and the job don't match. Identification does not mean "selling out" or lying.

It's time now for what Kenneth Burke would have called a representative anecdote.

After he had completed his qualifying examinations and was well under way on his dissertation, one of the brightest students I have ever known came into my office with this question: "What should I do to prepare for the job market?" My advice was this: Cut you hair, and get rid of your beaded headband. Get out of your thongs, holey blue jeans, and T-Shirt with its Rolling Stones emblem. Buy a pair of shoes, a pair of gray trousers, a white shirt, and a necktie. And wear them. He did. And he got a job.

Now the point is *not* that this student sold out to the establishment, but he did not, through his dress and manner, challenge interviewers to a fight. That is, by "talking their language" in the way he dressed, he invited them to discuss ideas and values with him. It is, I think, axiomatic that no one wins a fight as contrasted with a genuine argument, in which both sides listen and understand. In a real argument, everyone wins in that everyone gains new perspectives. In his "rhetoric," the student was (I hope) manifesting his commitment to one of academia's most cherished values: open-mindedness and the willingness to enter into dialogue. *Job Search in Academe* is a practical guide to entering the dialogue.

Formo and Reed may well have wrought better than they anticipated.

There is a world outside the academy. That is a truism that needs repeating. There is a world outside the academy (as Table 1 indicates). *Job Search in Academe* is a valuable resource for new and not-so-new Ph.D's and MA's who might look to careers in government, education, and business. Among my former students and old colleagues from graduate school, I number: a retired director of publications for a major aerospace firm; an executive with an international electronics firm; an assistant superintendent of schools; an owner of a large enterprise preparing documents for such corporations as Toyota; an executive with a large foundation; an associate director of a major research library; an assistant secretary of education.

It is, however, not obvious that a Ph.D in English, for instance, prepares one to fill the requirements of non-academic institutions. The new Ph.D in English has spent years writing and considering the nuances of language, but that writing has typically been nothing but literary term papers, and the language to which the graduate student has paid the most attention is that of "imaginative" expression. How many new Ph.D's in the humanities (or other fields) are aware of *Guidelines for Document Designers*, published by the American Institutes for Research? This publication is essential for anyone who intends to write funding proposals, sets of instructions, training manuals, brochures, and other "functional" documents. How many new Ph.D's in any field, but particularly in the humanities, have computer literacy that goes beyond the basics, word processing and internet search engines?

I am suggesting that some "extracurricular knowledge" can maximize the applicants' chances of obtaining a position—but not only outside academia. Envision the situation. Five hundred applications for one job at Utopia State University. The aspirants are from the whole range of institutions: state and private, less than prestigious and glitteringly so. All of the aspirants have gone through the requisite courses. All of them have teaching experience. In many ways all five hundred applicants are alike. Thus, if one of them has a background, a body of knowledge, or a skill that sets him or her apart from the rest, he or she has a distinct advantage. The ability to present oneself as competent in a variety of areas; skills that enable one to use computers as tools in advanced research; a background in public education, qualifying one to work with undergraduates who are preparing to be teachers—these are the sorts of assets that expand the field of job opportunities . . .

It seems to me that people working on doctorates are foolish if they do not seek ways to make themselves unique in what they have to offer prospective employers, either in or outside the academy.

Which brings me back to the subject of this foreword: *Job Search in Academe,* by Dawn M. Formo and Cheryl Reed. The candidate for a position needs the rhetorical skills to convince faculty committees or personnel directors that he or she does have unique abilities and knowledge. With a good deal of wit, with a whole lot of common sense, and with a sound grasp of the rhetoric of identification, Dawn M. Formo and Cheryl Reed have produced a "handbook" that will be invaluable to job seekers.

REFERENCE

Burke, Kenneth. *A Rhetoric of Motives.* 1962. Berkeley: U of California P, 1969.
MLA Newsletter (Summer 1998).

INTRODUCTION

Theor(ies): Becoming Literate in the Employment Line

Professor T. was great to talk to, but he admitted that his experience was very different than mine. He and I talked quite a bit about the problem of research university professors, who are generally the product of top-ten programs, who then turn around to advise students on the market for other kinds of institutions. He told me good stories about having half a dozen conference interviews and about barely missing some prestigious jobs, but his experience felt very far removed from what I was going through. In general, Professor T. was a friendly encourager, but he didn't give me vital information about what I would face in the search process.

—Assistant Professor

We REALLY need to have more access to each other's stories.

—Assistant Professor

Dr. Strangefield: Or, How We Learned to Stop Worrying and Love the Job Search[1]

If you intend to secure a job as an academic at a community college, teaching university, or research university, or if you are preparing graduate students for the academic job market, *Job Search* is for you. If you are a graduate student, you have spent years in graduate school looking forward with great anticipation to your life as a professional academic, but you have likely felt dissuaded by the discouraging academic job placement reports. If you are an adjunct faculty member, you may wonder if you will ever be able to secure a tenure-track position. If you are a faculty member, you are concerned about the lack of guidance graduate students receive in preparation for the job search. If you have picked up this book, you are fully aware that few graduate programs purposefully prepare their graduates for the academic job market. Job candidates just entering the job search usually feel (and are) underprepared. But graduate students and adjunct faculty certainly have the skills to be successful on the market, and faculty know that a little strategizing about the rhetorical situations job candidates encounter can greatly benefit their students as they enter the job market.

In *Job Search* we demonstrate that the job search process includes a range of rhetorical scenes, real-time moments that have distinct communication goals for the job candidate and the interviewer(s). This book assists faculty candidates and their advisors through the entire job search process including the application, the professional conference interview, the on-campus interview, and the contract signing. We call on our excessive (and expensive) rhetorical training as well as popular psycholinguistics, business-management theory, and the "lived experience" of successful job candidates in order to present some viable ways of becoming literate in the employment line. As rhetoricians, we devote special attention to the interview portion of the process.

After we discuss familiar theories that can help you become literate in the employment line in this introduction, we walk you through the job search in chapters 1 through 5, with chapter 4 focusing exclusively on unanticipated interview questions. In chapter 6, we invite you to read "success-story" vignettes from contributors who have secured satisfying academic and non-academic jobs. In the epilogue, we then encourage you to apply your experience to your own faculty candidate searches. Finally, the appendices offer useful resources:

- Resources for locating job announcements in many academic fields.
- Websites for finding non-academic positions.
- Information for designing a job search workshop for faculty candidates.

- Sample application letters for community college and university faculty positions and for a non-academic position.
- Sample *vitae* for community college and university faculty positions and a sample resume for a non-academic position.
- Suggested books and videos to help prepare for the academic job market.

Our Own Searches

When we applied to graduate school, we knew little about the projected job market. But we did know that our professors, the very ones who encouraged us to pursue graduate school, were confident that by the time we finished graduate work, the academic job market would be booming. In fact, Dawn recalls her undergraduate chair sketching out the economists' projections in the form of bar graphs, and Cheryl was told, "Even in a bad market, students like you get jobs." Our advisors saw great potential—in the job market and in us. While their words certainly encouraged us to attend graduate school, for some reason they also made us keep a wary eye on the *Modern Language Association (MLA) Job Information List* each year (which, as we now know, was not an encouraging activity). In fact, each year we wondered even more if we would ever be employed in this field. The words of optimism that launched our graduate careers were gone by the time we'd completed our coursework. Faculty comments about the market we'd face turned from excitement about the hopeful future to questions about university ethics in graduate school acceptance policies.

By 1994 (the year Dawn entered the market), the MLA job list was offering a slight boost to the confidence of those with composition/rhetoric training, with some 42.7 percent of the advertised jobs describing a need for those specializations. Ominously, however, *Profession '94* focused on the overall market's depressed (and depressing) prospects. At the University of Southern California, a lovably cantankerous W. Ross Winterowd suggested that the English department's acceptance letters to incoming graduate students note poor job market conditions. In 1995 (the year Cheryl took a selective leap into the fray), MLA President David T. Gies sadly remarked in his "Presidential Forum," "The job market looks bleak" (*Profession '95*, 5). In addition to the trying outlook, as we were applying for jobs, senior professors told us that many of the application packets that search committees receive today remind them of their first bids for tenure.

We approached this job search reality in slightly different ways. According to academic lore, Dawn entered the job market the "right way." She began her formal job search in October, applying only for positions listed in her field's job list (MLA). She submitted nearly fifty applications to universities around the country. In December, she interviewed at her field's national conference (MLA), accepted several invitations for campus interviews, and received two formal offers.

Cheryl took a non-traditional approach to the job market. She began teaching part time at a two-year college as soon as she completed all doctoral coursework and was invited to apply for full-time openings at both sites where she adjuncted. Avoiding MLA interviews as long as possible, she applied to two-year colleges and worked a self-fashioned "postdoc" in grant administration in a large university's department of psychiatry. She and her partner also performed an extensive demographic reconnaissance of cities likely to provide employment for her non-academic partner, as well. After rejecting one job offer and withdrawing her application from consideration in another, she reluctantly interviewed at the MLA, eventually succumbing to the lure of a tenure-track position at a state university. Dawn and Cheryl both secured tenure-track positions.

As we rehashed bewildering experiences in our own professional job searches, we began to ask ourselves why our training in rhetorical theory hadn't allowed us to "read" these situations more productively. Taking a page from our own discipline (rhetoric and composition), we began to analyze the job search as a series of rhetorical scenes. If, as we'd been taught, each interaction has an inherent rhetoric—a systemic logic, a way of assuming, implying, assessing, extrapolating, interpreting, and processing language, gesture, and intention within the context of the "lived experience" of its participants— could job seekers "unpack" the rhetorical structures operating in their own job searches?

We began to probe the interpretive strategies we had used intuitively during the process of our (ultimately successful) interview processes, and we asked other successful candidates to share narratives of their own job searches. What, we asked, makes each interview coherent as a narrative? Why is a particular question followed by a particular response? What is said? How is it said? Where is it said? Who says it? Why? What isn't said? What are the probable/actual outcomes of this interaction? And, perhaps not so theoretical, but nonetheless significant: How do the participants *feel*?

We began to think about search committee members as inhabitants of language communities. Their language acts (their speech to us and to each other) could give us rhetorical clues, we reasoned, about their relationship to their colleagues, their institutions, and the task of teaching/researching as a whole. We encountered a younger faculty member who "translated" the older chair's questions to the candidate, and the candidate's answers back to the chair; a faculty member who assumed all graduates from the candidate's school would turn down their first job offers; and a dean who used guilt to (attempt to) manipulate the interview schedule and presentation content. Our experience encouraged us to turn the tools of our discipline on our own professional experiences.

Specifically, we asked ourselves: What speaker roles are being presented to us in the interview setting? What do these roles say about how things get accomplished at this institution? What gets assumed, and what has to be explained to the characters quizzing us? Are committee members wooers, judges, cajolers, skeptics? Does one member of the committee act as a spokesperson, a translator, a heavy, an ingenue, a coach for the others? Then too, how is the candidate's role (both as an applicant and a potential colleague) being cast? Is the candidate a supplicant, a caretaker, a savior, a long shot? The ways in which a particular institution "casts its characters" can deeply affect the subjective experience of the academic interview, and, of course, the decisions made by all participants.

Trade publications in business communication and psycholinguistics resonated with our own search experiences before and behind the interview table. Some addressed strategies for dealing with situations likely to be encountered by target groups such as women, people of color, career changers, older job seekers, or recently "downsized" employees. Others addressed general concerns like making small talk, easing uncomfortable situations, and disagreeing with someone who has the power to decide your fate. Tongue firmly in cheek, these guides are written in a conversational style and brimming with anecdotal support and pithy, easily remembered sayings (important when you're under pressure to interpret a situation and make decisions on the spot). While we felt a bit sheepish checking out these self-help productions of the world of commerce, the experience-based, pragmatic advice these publications offered was well worth enduring the smiles and comments of the check-out librarian. Inevitably, we began to question how strange it was that no one prepared us for practicing this sort of "applied rhetoric." When we found Kate White's *Why Good Girls Don't Get Ahead . . . But Gutsy Girls Do* (our personal favorite among the general career guides), we knew we had to write a guide for the *faculty* job seeker.

Applied Rhetorics: Becoming Literate in the Employment Line

Time and again different theorists have noted how knowledge production is a social enterprise, and that the selection mechanisms as to what gets taught and who gets educated are not fair. That they are, in fact, deeply intertwined with existing structures of power.

But somehow, the tone that comes through in many job search narratives is a mix of surprise and entitlement betrayed. Graduate students in my field who have argued for years that the existing social structures are oppressive are nonetheless surprised when they don't get "good jobs." Students who have spent much time critiquing meritocracy still expect it to select them as the best.

—*Greg Beatty, Online Educator*

Whereas critical trends like cultural studies, Marxism, and deconstruction were the craze in graduate school, at the undergraduate institutions where I interviewed, faculty members were more interested in the candidate's love of the subject, and in less radical theoretical approaches that worked well in the undergraduate classroom.

—*Assistant Professor Jennifer C. Vaught*

In our own discipline of composition and rhetoric, and in many of the humanities, a number of studies have shown how bad things are in terms of academic employment. The discussions of these results revolve around statistics, but no one seems to be giving a systematic reading of the rhetoric of each of the components that make up the search. In *Job Search*, our interest is not so much in the fact that there is a market crisis or in the numbers that go along with that. Those sorts of analyses simply point out that a problem exists but leave it relatively intact. Our project is to break open all the interlocking components of the job search process to see what drives it rhetorically and to offer specific suggestions for navigating the market.

METHODOLOG(IES)

To understand the language acts and communities that operate within the academic search process, *Job Search* combines feminism's tradition of valuing the personal with postmodern rhetoric's reading of the cultural and the historical. We apply our extensive (and expensive) training in rhetoric to real-time interactions and academic search lore in order to offer a theoretical reading of—and practical guide to—the current job market.

VALORIZING THE PERSONAL

Feminists have long argued that personal experience is not a set of random, unconnected scenes, but rather creates the framing stories of the cultures we inhabit.[2] In the interview process, then, a sequence of rhetorical scenes creates professionally personal moments. Throughout the interview process, theory gets applied in real-time moments that can affect the outcome of all those years of training in theory and research methodology.

We collected over sixty personal narratives through face-to-face, tape-recorded interviews and through electronic responses to two calls we sent over the Internet to faculty (tenured and untenured), administrators, and graduate students in the sciences, social sciences, and humanities. The contributors represent a cross-section of fields including the humanities, social sciences, sciences, and business. They came from research universities, teaching colleges and universities, and community colleges. In collecting their narratives, our research goal was not to make a valid statistical sample or even to present "lived experience," but rather to draw upon the expertise that's being let lay fallow in our current system. Analyzing the rhetorical structures underlying these experiences was our blatant attempt to include the real-life struggles and successes of job holders and job seekers in the making of a book that discussed the real-world job market. In order to collect the greatest number of meaningful responses to our call for narratives, we offered acknowledgement options to the contributors: anonymity or full citation for professional recognition. The fact that many of our contributors wished to remain anonymous points to the risky political climate of the job search. We've used names and titles wherever possible but some of our contributors asked to remain anonymous since they were explaining situations that could reflect badly on the institutions at which they interviewed or trained. We hope that we've been successful in modifying identifying markers so that no one recognizes him or herself in these pages.

Job Search, then, does not attempt to do a statistical study of job searching or an analysis of market conditions. Instead, our book embeds the real-life language acts of job seekers within an investigation of productive strategies for the academic job search.

LEARNING FROM LORE

Many of our contributors embedded savvy strategies and pointed advice for the academic job seeker in their comments and narratives. This "insider" counsel constitutes what compositionist Louise Wetherbee Phelps has called "lore": a disciplinary storytelling that translates collective experience from one set of savvy individuals to the up-and-coming.[3] Medicine has long used the narrative of experience to transfer information in its use of case studies. Kathryn Hunter, for instance, notes that "doctors' stories" pass insider knowledge along from seasoned doctors to interns: case studies require respondents to look at the complexity of a given situation (or case) framed as a story. The lore of a profession, it seems, teaches us to apply rational criteria in a flexible way that accounts for the complexity of human experience.

Whether we intuit them or not, we all operate in social narrative streams. Each institution has a personality: students, mission statements, and the disciplinary content create the lore of collective experience, thereby defining what it means to work in a particular place. In other words, there's a whole lot of truth-telling in the hallway chatter. *Job Search* promises to help you prepare for the full application-to interview job search by looking at this narrative and theoretical advice-giving.

TURNING RHETORIC INTO STRATEGY

Many graduate students are taught to question ideological structures rather aggressively. What compositionists call the "dialectic" approach in essence turns any conversation or piece of writing into an investigation of hidden motives and attempts by one conversant to shut down choice for the other. For example, a dialectic approach to the book you're holding in your hand would have you question our motives in giving you advice: Are we trying to make money or tenure from *your* job search? Are we trying to get you to conform to some arbitrary consensus of standards for employed academics? While questions like these sound ludicrous in this context—after all, no matter what *our* motives are, the strategies in this book could help *you* get a job— we've found surprisingly similar illogic in the language and behaviors of many faculty job candidates.

Many candidates don't realize that the job interview is a completely different rhetorical situation from the graduate seminar debate, one in which the goal is to construct rather than tear down. The very contestation that works so well in debate around the graduate seminar table is suicidal in a situation that requires connection. If you've been inundated with an inherently contestatory methodology for critique over the past few years, chances are you'll carry a very unproductive "dialectic" strategy into your own job search.

Consider the competitive language acts that characterize many graduate school classrooms. In the competitive, "dialectic" project, we learn to look at individual acts as indicators of larger social structures that feed destructive ideologies such as racism, sexism, classism, and nationalism. Unfortunately, when real-time job seekers carry the dialectic project into their job searches, they almost inevitably engage every language interaction as a forum where logical flaws are publicly exposed so that confining structures can be dismantled. They thereby miss the inherently constructive—or "dialogic"— task which should structure the interview exchange.

We increasingly sense that language communities are inhabited and continually reformulated by individuals with particularized histories, working within peculiar juxtapositions of empowerment and dis/ability much more complex (and exciting) than any set of critiques can deal with honestly or adequately. While the dialectical, contestatory approach certainly leads to interesting research, carrying this classroom project into the interview process can make you critique—rather than build connections to—the very institution you hope to join. To pull apart structures when you are trying to construct a relationship (or at least a discussion about a possible relationship) is sure failure. In fact one science contributor explains, "Unfortunately, I have seen graduate students who have learned that tearing apart information is all there is to being an effective researcher, and they lose sight of their roles as teachers." Ironically, many candidates botch their job searches by continuing to employ the very strategies that have gained them glowing recommendation letters.

In *Job Search*, we pose the interview process as collaborative, connective, or "dialogic"—an opportunity for the participants to work together to construct meaning and to create a negotiated understanding of the professional relationship.[4] We won't tell you how to critique or even reproduce any of the limiting structures you may have discussed as part of your graduate training. Rather, this job guide shows you how to negotiate the structures that are already in place, structures that affect and orchestrate what you can do with the stunning intellectual critiques you've been trained to make of those structures.

ON TO SUCCESS

One of our colleagues in the sciences tells us that candidates in her field should be particularly comfortable with the variables of the job search because they are used to investigating the unknown. Basic disciplinary training, it seems, invites science candidates to approach the job search as a series of procedures which yield predictable and reproducible results. Another science colleague disagrees: science majors do fine at data interpretation, she told us, but "political or social variables thrown into the mix equal a big problem." These witty colleagues, like the many contributors you'll meet in the next few pages, crafted their own understanding and negotiation of the job market, approaches that express their own cognitive styles and life experiences.

These contributors from across the disciplines—many of them graduate students now on the market—are already "star" players. Savvy, innovative, and passionate about the pressing issues of their disciplines, they're intuitively (or consciously) recognizing and responding to the job search as a set of rhetorical scenes. The contributors who are already enjoying faculty positions have shown us that successful candidates know that the interview process requires particular kinds of skills not taught, valorized, or encouraged in the graduate classroom. Although these faculty candidates may not call it applied rhetoric, on "the market" they are doing what rhetorical theory claims as its rightful domain.

In *Job Search*, our goal is not to offer tools for out-maneuvering the interviewer, but to suggest that you are performing within a different set of scenes from those your graduate training prepared you for. *Job Search* is not an exposé, as one (rejected) publisher hoped we would produce. Rather, traditional rhetorical theory combined with real people's voices makes visible the unacknowledged language structures underlying the academic job search. The very qualified and capable scholars who are our contributors have already caught on to the fact that one rhetorical tool—argumentation—will not fit all rhetorical scenes. They have already intuited the need to switch from the dialectic (contestatory) model of intellectual one-upmanship to the dialogic (collaborative) model that negotiates meaning and builds relationship.

If you're still wondering whether *Job Search* is for you, read on! Here's to your successful preparation for, and success in, the academic job market.

NOTES

1. Thanks to Samuel Reed for his witty suggestion for this section title, based on the 1964 film starring Peter Sellers, *Dr. Strangelove: or, How I Learned to Stop Worrying and Love the Bomb.* The movie depicts a culture learning to deal with the potential for survival after protracted nuclear battles, a metaphor we find strangely compelling.

2. Susan C. Jarratt's, Dale Bauer's, Audre Lorde's, and Karla F. C. Halloway's scholarship collectively suggests a path out of the dialectic/dialogic ideological dilemma. We can use their emphasis on proactive, ethically-grounded rhetoric to enable ourselves to make the professional conversations in which we engage productive.

3. See Louise Wetherbee Phelps's *Composition as a Human Science: Contributions to the Self-Understanding of a Discipline.* New York: Oxford UP, 1988.

4. The shared conversation between the interviewers and the interviewee should represent what language theorists identify as a "Burkean Parlour." See Kenneth Burke's *A Rhetoric of Motives.* 1962. U of California P, 1969.

I

WRITING THE SCRIPT
The Application Process

Finding and Interpreting the Job Announcement

Faculty positions are routinely announced in disciplinary journals, academic news publications like *The Chronicle of Higher Education*, websites like those supported by C-C-FEST Lingua Moo (an academic virtual community at http://lingua.utdallas.edu:7000/2194), annual job lists such as the *Job Opportunities for Economists* (*JOE*), which is issued solely to announce the year's openings, and flyers mass-mailed to departments or distributed at conferences (see appendix 1, "Finding a Job Announcement in Your Field"). If you find an ad in a smaller publication aimed at a specialized group or region, check if the position is also being advertised in the standard job listings for your field. One search committee member reported that citing a position announcement from a national job list indicated that the candidate was "serious" enough to be aware of the official organs of his or her field. On the other hand, ads that are circulated regionally, not nationally, imply a certain expectation that all candidates will be in easy, inexpensive travelling distance for interviews and that they will be in tune with the concerns of the region. If you are interested in a position that has narrowed its field of candidates in this way, give some thought as to how you can frame in your application materials your interest in that institution and geographic region.

The language in these announcements generally adheres scrupulously to that mandated in federally monitored hiring guidelines. (Exceptions to this occur when a school is privately funded and receives no government monies; however, the wording varies remarkably little, even in these cases.) Most announcements are terse, giving the bare bones of information about the position and (most importantly) what materials the applicant should send, and where to send them. Abbreviations like "ABD" ("all but dissertation) and "3-2-2 teaching load" (teaching three courses in the first quarter and two courses in each remaining quarter) are rampant. Many simply ask for a "dossier" or "application materials," terms that can be interpreted in such different ways that the candidate may wonder whether or not a writing sample or letters of recommendation should be included.

Casie Hermansson, the graduate student who co-organized the interview workshop included in our appendix, recalls her first look at these ads:

> When I looked at the job announcements, the abbreviations seemed cabalisitic at best, and I had little hope of interpreting between their lines. I concluded that in order to make best use of time and money when I had the 'earned' doctorate 'in hand' I needed to approach the process as I would a course. It was going to need regular time, research, savings, and practice.

The purpose of the job announcement is simply to announce the potential of a job opening at the institution cited. It's the initial overture in a very long conversation. Here are some things you need to know about interpreting job announcements:

- Beyond an opening in a particular discipline, the position announcement may not reflect the specific desires of the search committee or even of the hiring department.

- The position announced may not yet have received budget approval, Jennifer C. Vaught, Assistant Professor at a regional university, points out. Because of publication deadlines for the job lists and the cycle of interviews at annual disciplinary conferences, many institutions have to submit advertisements for positions that may not ultimately materialize.

- Openings at large, interconnected state schools are the tip of the iceberg: late-breaking openings may cause applications for a position at one campus to be recycled to other interested campuses.

- Degree status and other positioning labels may be institution-specific. In one candidate's experience, for example, reviewers questioned her use of the term "Candidate in Philosophy." Although "Candidate" meant the same thing as "ABD" at her degree-granting institution, this term caused confusion and even suspicion with some reviewers as to whether or not she had finished the required coursework.

- Terms used in the position announcements, themselves, may not be as clear as they seem. What, for instance, is "a fixed-term position?" How is this different from an "adjunct?" What is "indefinite tenure?" How does it compare to "tenure-track?" These terms are meaningful to the people who wrote the ads, but you shouldn't feel backward for not knowing what they mean. While it is probably not a good idea to deluge the respective campuses with inquisitive phone calls at this preliminary stage, clarifying these terms is definitely something you want to do during the interview.

Your first step, then, is to be sure you know what you're applying for. Alan Kalish, Director of the Center for Teaching and Learning at California State University, Sacramento, concludes from his research into successful hires that "realistic expectations for both how the job search process works and what [a new hire] would face" in an entry-level position make the transition from graduate student to faculty member much less trying for all concerned. Consider carefully, then, what the job ad does tell you. How does the institution describe itself? the opening? your specialization? Is there play in the areas of specialization that qualify you for the opening? In other words, are they hard-wired into one description, or does the ad indicate that many different combinations of subspecialties will be considered? Is teaching or community service stressed? Are words like "proactive," "innovative," or "motivated" used to describe the ideal candidate? Are qualifiers or disclaimers like "expecting to receive approval," or "potential for extended funding" sprinkled throughout a relatively short ad? Does the ad suggest why an opening has occurred—a sabbatical replacement, a new program, the result of increases in a particular student population? Or, as Associate Professor of Humanities Michael Day points out, would you really want to live in the geographic area designated in the announcement?

Although job announcements follow rather formulaic language structures, they are your first best indication of how an institution imagines an open position. Virginia Carroll, Associate Professor of English at Kent State University, recommends that candidates "read the job description carefully and make an argument that your qualifications fit: if a job emphasizes teaching, for example, the standard letter with two paragraphs of details about the dissertation topic and a sentence about teaching doesn't make sense." Therefore, craft your application materials to show how your training, experience and personal style would work in the context the ad sets up.

The Application Packet as a Rhetorical Scene

The first exchange of information between you and potential new colleagues will be on paper—and it will be an exchange much mediated by bureaucratic "others." In fact, since most applications are opened and sorted by a departmental staffperson and/or funneled through the human resources office, the first person who touches your packet will most likely be someone with training in administrative support, rather than in your discipline.

The person who initially handles your application, then, may or may not have been trained in the areas in which you've immersed yourself the past few years of your life. In fact, he or she may be armed only with a list of categories under which to sort the deluge of applicants for multiple advertised positions. The sorting rubric may be as simple as "arrived before deadline" or "meets minimum degree requirements," but institutions which have multiple sites and multiple positions open may establish a particular search committee for each opening. In this case (as in one large West Coast school) an office staffperson may have to decide which committee(s) should see a particular application. Make this person's job easy: format your materials so that training, experience, and desired position are easy to find, and use headers and job titles that reflect the language of the position announcement (see appendix 4 for sample application materials). Please note that the application process costs you money. Expect that with the cost of transcripts, postage, and paper that you will spend anywhere from $5–10 per application.

At the "paper" stage of the search process, your main task is to begin constructing your professional presence or, as Jungians might say, your "persona." There is nothing counterfeit about the personas you construct for your applications, although laying down something as complex as lived experience in a few short pages can feel that way. Think of your application packet as a preliminary script, one that sketches out the role you want to play once you get a chance "on stage" at your hiring university. Your interpretation and development of this role will be slightly (or even significantly) different than that of other candidates, and the way a particular university stages its "productions" will also affect the kind of performance you can offer.

Psycholinguist Suzette Elgin analyzes the modes and metaphors of verbal presentation in her Gentle Art of Verbal Self-Defense series (see especially *GenderSpeak* and *BusinessSpeak*). This trade series offers ways to hear the message all-too-often obscured by a method of presentation, to avoid unproductive exchanges, and to respond to the content, rather than the mode, of a message. Elgin also suggests that we watch for the metaphors we, ourselves, use intuitively to describe given relationships, because we tend to enact these metaphors. In the context of the job search, for example, a candidate might slip into a lovelorn metaphor, in which (s)he has projected an attractive image to many prospective partners (the application process) and now sits home waiting for the phone to ring (the follow-up call) in order to find that one true match, to be someone's "chosen one" (the job offer). Compare this thread with a business metaphor: The applicant has assembled and distributed the portfolio to several viable prospects (the application process), and is now anticipating potential colleagues' feedback on their proposed collaboration (the follow-up call) so that (s)he can establish a productive base of operations to pursue personal career goals (the job offer). Verbal style, assumed roles, and implicit metaphors reflect underlying attitudes that ultimately affect the way we present very important things such as training, experience, and specialization.

Your paper "persona," then, will look a bit different for each job opening, as you will be presenting key aspects of your training, experience, and intellectual focus within the context of a particular job opening, and according to your metaphoric "reading" of your own candidacy. Yet, each application, as distinct from the others as it may be, should accurately portray who you are in the professional context. Each application packet will also present several perspectives of this professional persona:

- Who are you as a teacher? as a researcher? (the *vita* and recommendation letters)

- What do your mentors think of you? (the recommendation letters)

- How do you present yourself? How do you interpret your own interests and training in light of the advertised job? (the application letter)

And, probably the hardest to get across—

* How are you different from all the other candidates applying for the same job?

Start thinking of yourself as a colleague (not a supplicant or a thesis defender) now, when potential face-to-face interactions with the search committee are still in the realm of the imaginary. This doesn't mean, of course, that you will present yourself as a peer; becoming a peer is the primary task of the tenure-track years. Neither will you imply that you are God's gift to the university ("Act now and you can snap me up before I accept a more prestigious offer!"). After all, as an entry-level applicant you are hoping to become the most junior member of whichever faculty you propose to join. But you do want to propose yourself as a serious contender for that most junior position, someone who is ready to step into a full-tilt, demanding schedule and perform well. How, then, do you select what to include in each packet? The application packet generally consists of an application letter, a curriculum vita (c.v.), and several letters of recommendation, although schools may initially ask for only candidate-generated materials (the application letter and c.v.). Confidential recommendation letters describe your accomplishments from the perspectives of your mentors. The *vita* lists your accomplishments and training by category—education, publications, presentations, teaching experience and interests, grants and awards, and references. The application letter briefly contextualizes key items within the specific parameters of the job for which you're applying. Each of these components not only help win you an "audition," but also can help you prepare for interviews that result. While occasionally hiring committees will ask short-listed candidates for writing samples, lesson plans, student evaluations, or even teaching videos, don't send these materials until you're asked to, or unless your particular discipline has specific expectations. Search committees read up to hundreds of applications for each opening and generally don't appreciate unsolicited additions to their reading load.

The Curriculum Vitae

Oddly enough, given the ease of formatting offered by even the most rudimentary word-processing software, many applicants prepare *vitae* that visually obscure important information about their personal fit for the job opening. While, of course, an attractively-formatted *vita* won't get you an interview if your training and experience don't favorably impress readers, a clear format can certainly help your readers find the information they need to make a favorable assessment.

USING FORMATTING TO MAKE A VISUAL ARGUMENT

The curriculum vitae is the most visual element of your application packet, and also the piece most readers turn to when first assessing whose application to keep, and whose to cut. Give some serious thought, then, to how you use white space, bolding, block text, header placement and graphics. You want the reader's eye to bounce quickly from one key item to the next:

- Who is this? (name, contact address, institutional affiliations)
- Is (s)he qualified for this opening? (degrees awarded)
- What has (s)he done in the field? (experience, publications)
- Who can tell me more about him/her? (references)

And then back to the beginning:

- Who is this? how can we contact him/her?

The first and last thing you want the reader to remember is clearly your name—so be sure it's easy to find (and read). There are many devices you can use to do this; one of the simplest is centering your name at the top of the *vita* rather than following the customary business letter format of including it in the address block:

Your Name

Street Address	School Address
City, State, Zip	Department
	City, State, Zip
Phone	School phone
Email	

You can also use a slightly larger font size (if the *vita* is set in 12, for instance, your name could appear in 14 or 16), and bold it:

Your Name

If your level of training is particularly important—for example, if you have a Ph.D. and many candidates for the same position may simply have M.A.'s— you might include that after your name:

Your Name, Ph.D.

You might even want to set the information about how to contact you apart from the rest of the *vita* with discrete graphics:

Y o u r   N a m e , P h . D.

Home Address	School Address
City, State, Zip	Department
	City, State, Zip
Phone	School phone
Email	

Degrees Awarded

1998	Ph.D.	Composition and Rhetoric	University of Quixote
1993	M.A.	English	State College

Note that the first section header after the contact information— "Degrees Awarded"—is, like the candidate's name, bolded. Bolding section headers and setting them apart visually by using white space (i.e., by skipping to the next line to start detailing information pertinent to that section) will help the reader's eye dance down the page from one section to the next, gathering the *vita*'s "argument" that you're a viable candidate for this position along the way. Naturally, there are other formatting devices that allow you to do this; the key here is to set up information about your training, experience, publications, and contact addresses in a format that can be quickly scanned and easily assimilated by the many harried viewers of your life's work to date.

Keep in mind that your application materials will most likely be photocopied and passed around endlessly among many sets of reviewers, from file clerks who handle them as just another task to do before lunch, to committee members, to administrators, and back again. Thus, expensive stationery-quality or specially-tinted paper will most likely go unappreciated (not only will the original sit in the file clerk's office, but unusual textures or colors can result in some really bad photocopies to under-whelm search committee members). Our more technologically oriented colleagues speculate that the application process will eventually become electronic, and involve its own rhetoric, dictated by the limitations of software and hardware in use.

In fact, one of our contributors who teaches business writing argues, "Given the intense time pressures of the academic job search, especially if a department wants to interview someone at their discipline's conference, electronic versions of a *vita* and a cover letter may make sense." Assistant Professor of English Marcy Tanter adds her electronic job search experience:

> I just got a job and a large part of how I got it has to do with the Internet. I first found out about it through a listserv and kept in constant email contact with the chair of the hiring committee. Although I'm absolutely qualified for the position, I'm sure that if it weren't for the emailing, I wouldn't have a job now.

An assistant professor of chemistry adds:

> We were most impressed with a recent candidate who had his own web site and discussed personal and professional goals very candidly. The web site included more detailed info than the *vita*, and it was definitely slanted to land a position in physical chemistry (not what we were hiring!).

If you're electronically savvy, use these resources! They can help you keep in contact with key decision makers and they can augment and enhance your application packet. Keep in mind, however, that these very public documents should show your entire range of teaching and research abilities so that you don't accidentally dazzle yourself out of a job.

ARRANGING THE INFORMATION ON YOUR CURRICULUM VITAE

As strange as it may seem, the order in which you present your background information can also play a telling role in how your *vita* (and candidacy) gets read. Early in her job search, one of the authors arranged her *vita* to foreground her teaching experience, relegating her publications list to the last pages of the *vita* in order to avoid clutter and to show that she prioritized teaching. This strategy had an unexpected effect: in order to cut costs, department personnel at one institution copied and distributed only the first page of an applicant's *vita*. Thus, during telephone interviews, search committee members who hadn't seen her healthy publications list repeatedly asked why she hadn't made the effort to publish! Marked as an "underperformer" in one conversation after another, she eventually canceled her campus interview, feeling unable to correct the search committee's set impressions. While of course this experience says more about confusion, budget constraints, and personalities at that particular institution than it does about any *vita* format, giving people what they expect, in the order they expect it, can go a long way to minimizing such mystifying readings of your *vita*.

Just what order do people expect a *vita* to follow? Consider the information the search committee needs to "build a case" for your candidacy. Here are the questions search committee members most often report having in mind as they peruse the different sections of your *vita*:

- Does the candidate have the Ph.D. or specialty license in hand? If not, how close is (s)he? (Degrees/Licensure Awarded)

- What's his/her area of specialization? (Dissertation Title and Interests)

- How will this candidate's research interests enrich my own research, or lessen the teaching load of faculty in this institution? Does this candidate have a fair chance of producing tenurable work, so we don't have to go through the search process again soon? (Publications and Presentations List)

- Has this person taught students like ours before, either under supervision or, better yet, as the sole instructor for/creator of the course? (Teaching Experience)

- How can this candidate lessen my own workload? (Other Academic Experience, Teaching Interests, Service Interests)

- Do I know (of) anyone (s)he's worked with? Has (s)he had good mentoring? What kinds of people are willing to support this applicant's work record? (Reference List)

The authors have served on search committees that actually checked specific categories off on a grid of expectations, then ranked each candidate according to how many check marks each had racked up. Take a look at the following sample *vita* —geared to a teaching-oriented institution—and gauge how it makes accessible key categories of information. If this were a *vita* directed toward a more research-oriented position, "Service Interests" would most likely be replaced by "Research Interests."

Applicant's Name

Contact address	Alternate contact address
City, State, Zip code	[usually an institutional affiliation]
Area code, contact phone number	
E-mail address [if desired]	

Degrees and Licensure Awarded

Date	Degree/License Concentrations	Institution Awarding Degree/License

Dissertation

Title
Committee Members: Name, title

Grants and Awards

Date	Title of Award

Teaching Interests	**Service Interests**
Short list	Short List

Academic Publications [Use italics for manuscripts accepted for publication, but not yet in print. Add "forthcoming" after entry.]

"Title," *Journal* Volume (Date): page numbers.

Presentations

"Title." Name of Conference Month, Day, Year of Conference.

Works in Progress [Note: if your field is particularly cutthroat, leave this section out.]

"Title," type of project [book, article, translation, dissertation revision, etc.].

Teaching Experience

Dates Worked   Job Title
Description of your unique contributions to the generic job description.

Other Academic Experience [include administrative, editorial, or other non- teaching experience]

Dates worked   Job or Activity Title

Description of your unique contributions to the generic job description.

References

Name, Title
Institutional Affiliation
Address
City, State, Zipcode
Area Code, Office Phone Number

As you can see, a well-crafted *vita* visually and structurally builds an argument for potential interviewers about who and where you are (including professional titles, if applicable), how long you've trained, what hands-on experience you've had, how you've participated in the field, and who can give an "insider's" perspective of your work. Virginia Carroll points out that typos and errors "give the impression (fair or not) that the candidate is either unprofessional, unskilled at written communication, or inattentive to details." The clearer and more accessible you can make this information, the better.

HOW TO PRESENT KEY INFORMATION

There are some rather strange conventions connected with *vitae* reading that you should know about, because these will affect how the information you offer gets read in a given context. Because you will be one of many candidates for any given position, and because search committee members will be performing all the time-consuming tasks involved in a major search in addition to their regular teaching/service/research loads, make sure the wording in each *vita* category is excruciatingly clear and easily remembered. Your *vita* should indicate, as the saying goes, that you are "unique, just like everyone else." In other words, the information you present should clearly indicate that you fit the job criteria, while also offering memorable "sound bites" about special traits you alone can bring to the position.

Here are suggestions how to avoid common mistakes *vita* writers make:

- **Degrees/Licensure Awarded** Modesty would tell you that, if you don't yet have your Ph.D. or specialty license in hand, you shouldn't list it on the *vita*— or perhaps that you should list it as "forthcoming." However, these practices tend to signal that you, yourself, doubt you will finish your dissertation work in time to take on the demanding full-time positions for which you're applying. List your Ph.D.-to-be as if you already have it, even if the date shows its culmination to be months in the future. Ironically, this setup signals your firm intention to follow through rather than stopping at the M.A. or ABD (All But Dissertation):

- **Degrees Awarded**

2004	Ph.D.	Literature	University of the Hills
1999	B.A.	English	State College

- **Grants and Awards** Again, while common sense would dictate that you omit instances where people gave you money or fame (after all, that says more about their generosity than anything else, doesn't it?), naming grants and awards indicates that other people have thought enough of your work to actually fund it or reward it somehow. No grant is too small; in fact, one of the authors was asked during an important interview about a grant she'd received years earlier as a nascent community college student. Similarly, membership in academic organizations like the National Council of Teachers of English (NCTE) show—not simply that you mailed your dues in on time— but that you're already identifying yourself as a player in that field. If you belong to prestigious scholarly organizations, especially ones that add members by invitation only, you may want to create a header like Professional Affiliations.

- **Academic Publications and Presentations** When you're just starting out, you may not have enough publications to list them separately from your presentations. A general header like "Publications and Presentations" works well in this case. Once each list grows, you will want a separate list for each category. Use the standard bibliographic documentation format in your field minus the author portion. If you don't, your publication list will beat the reader over the head with repetition of the obvious:

Reed, Cheryl. "Steady as She Goes: The Tenure-Track Balancing Act," National Women's Studies Association Conference, Oswego, NY. June 9-12, forthcoming.

Reed, Cheryl. "Just Listening: Neuropsychobiology and Autobiography." Re-covering the Past. 95h Annual Conference of the Department of Romance Languages and Literatures, Binghampton University, April 17–18, 1998.

Reed, Cheryl. "Technology's Dark Side." Teaching in the Community College Online Conference, April. 7–9, 1998.

Reed, Cheryl. "Working Without a Net: Making Connections in the Non-Electronic Classroom." Reprinted in *Background Readings*. Ed. Susan Naomi Bernstein. Ancillary for *Real Writing: Paragraphs and Essays for College, Work, and Everyday Life*. ed. Susan Anker. Boston: Bedford Books, 1998.

Reed, Cheryl and Dawn M. Formo. "Service Learning in the Writing Class," editorial. *The Writing Instructor*. 16.2 (Winter 1997): 51–52.

Cheryl's father, a Texas rancher, would call this an "operatic" presentation ("Me-Me- Me-Me-Meeee!"). Better to omit your name and start each entry with the title. If you have co-written or copresented a piece, omit your name and supply your co-author's name in parentheses:

(with Dawn M. Formo). "Service Learning in the Writing Class," editorial. *The Writing Instructor*. 16.2 (Winter 1997): 51–52.

• **Teaching Experience** Use one or two lines of description that set you apart from all the other people who have the same job title. Be as specific as possible here. How many sections, of which classes, at what level, did you teach? Did you write your own syllabi? Did you develop standard projects in an innovative way? Did you or your students win awards?

• **Other Academic Experience** This is where you'll list experience and activities that prepared you in some way to make a unique contribution to the job(s) for which you're applying. As in the Teaching Experience section, you can describe the skills and professional qualities your work as a test reader, conference organizer, journal editor, or tutoring center staffperson displays.

If you're part of an academic couple, admitting this in your application packet is not a good strategy. That information comes best later in the search process. An associate professor at West Coast University tells us of her experience:

> I think as assistant professors you have to hide being part of an academic couple. We wanted to be honest about being an academic couple. We applied for all positions that had two or more openings. We sent out materials together in the same envelope with individual envelopes inside. We sent a cover letter that said we are separate but together. I don't think it was a good approach. We didn't even get a preliminary interview with many of these. For those announcements where there was only one position and only one of us applied, we had a greater success rate. I think we were shooting ourselves in the foot applying as a couple.

As another anonymous contributor's experience suggests, it is difficult to know when to inform interviewers that you are part of an academic couple. After a private think tank offered her a prominent, extremely well-paid position in AIDS research and actively courted her to join their project she casually mentioned discussing the offer with her husband, and the recruitment died a sudden death. The prestigious think tank precipitously withdrew their offer to her. By that time, her partner, a chemist, had obtained a tenure-track position at an East Coast university, so the couple decided not to press the issue.

We certainly wish that we had more sage advice to offer academic couples. As one of our readers pointed out, the question about when and where to mention that you are part of an academic couple is a tricky question to answer. Unfortunately, no one can give you that answer. Every job situation is different. Institutional decisions to hire an applicant's spouse will likely be based on current needs and funding at a particular institution and on the specialization of the academic partner. Our best advice, as we tell you in chapter 5, is to collect all of the information you can about a situation. Then do what feels comfortable to you.

Couples in which only one partner is an academic may face much the same dilemma. If a university is the main employer in the area, your non-academic partner may not be able to find adequate (or soul-satisfying) work. At the time of this writing, at least one of our contributors was contemplating leaving a tenure-track position in a small town that could not support her partner's career. We have no easy answers for this, but would advise you to explore the job prospects your partner may have in an area as part of your on-campus interview. Your interviewers will be under constraints *not* to raise this issue, so it will be up to you to ask questions about the area economy, the job prospects in your non-academic partner's field, and even regional housing and food costs. This information can be collected quite naturally as you're touring the area with search committee members and should not cause any raised eyebrows. In fact, it may come as a relief to search committee members who would like to make you aware of regional dilemmas, but feel that broaching the subject would wander on to forbidden ground about living arrangements.

You and your partner may be able to strategize compromises if a particular regional economy can only support one of your careers. Many of the non-academic partners we spoke to had, in fact, "reinvented" themselves in unexpected ways in the face of under-employment. Whether or not these compromises are ultimately soul-satisfying depends, of course, on the career goals both partners hold, and on the inner workings of the relationship.

THE PRE-PRINTED APPLICATION FORM

If you're requested to fill out a standard corporate-style application form (as many community colleges do), take this request seriously. Even though this type of application form looks like the ones you filled out for your summer jobs at fast-food restaurants, don't simply fill in the blanks with "see *vita*." Give some thought to re-presenting the standard application materials in this more compact format. The departmental secretary or the human resources office may use this form instead of your *vita* or letter to determine who next sees your packet. An administrative assistant may check certain institution-specific blocks of information, perhaps even counting the number of credit hours, graduate composition courses, or writing classes taught, to determine your baseline eligibility for the position advertised.

If you are very accomplished, you will not have room on a pre-printed form simply to reproduce the information presented on your *vita*. You will need to decide how to present a great deal of information in a very small space, without leaving awkward gaps in the process. Perhaps the easiest way to accomplish this is to think in terms of categories instead of painstakingly chronological listings of experience. If, for example, you have published journal articles and similarly impressive work, but your latest output is a series of reviews, don't fill up the available spaces on your application form with a strict chronological listing which gives the impression you've only published reviews. Likewise, if the form allows you three spaces to present appropriate teaching experience, make sure you use those three, pre-printed spaces to show an *accurate* record of your *overall* teaching history *relevant for the announced job opening.* Did you teach at the community college or secondary level before beginning work on your Ph.D.? Did you leave a teaching position to pursue an interesting research project? Don't let strict chronology or awkward forms prevent you from stating relevant experience or training. The job announcement, itself, offers you a concise lexicon of terms to use in presenting your qualifications. Repeating these terms on the pre-printed forms will not only help you make use of limited space, it will make your candidacy immediately "legible" to the people who will be sorting your materials.

Your main goal in the pre-printed form is to be accurate and complete in a very small space. Once you've completed the pre printed form's block cat egories, it's perfectly appropriate to add, "See attached *vita* for additional experience/publications/training." Some forms even instruct you to add additional pages if your experience overflows their parameters. Even though this means retyping your *vita* to match the form's format, do so. Taking the pre-printed application form seriously, then, means attention to the following formatting characteristics:

- Like the clearly-formatted *vita*, the complete pre-printed form is neatly presented. Don't hurriedly scrawl illegible, unintelligible answers in its too-small blanks. Locate a high-quality typewriter and take some time to insert Xs in appropriate boxes, and to center information on the lines provided.

- Although brief to the point of being telegraphic, the data you provide on the pre-printed form is accurate. Check dates, numbers and types of courses required in your own coursework, numbers and types of courses taught, and any other quantitative data the pre-printed form requests.

- (Most importantly), the pre-printed form frames your experience, training, and desired position in the language and phrasing of the job announcement itself. Since the job announcement will most likely be used as a rubric for sorting applications received, make sure your application form shows how well you fit that rubric. You can elaborate on fine points and subgenres of disciplinary focus later, when you're addressing the search committee.

Taking care with the pre-printed form will get your materials to the appropriate committee members for preliminary sorting.

How to Write Application Letters

The application letter shouldn't merely summarize your *vita*. The letter is the place to expand on the *vita*'s pithy lists, to explain connections, and to talk about the aptitudes and insights you gained from your experience as a graduate student and instructor. Bring out any administrative or community service aspects of your graduate experience—curriculum development, organization of orientation sessions, TA (teaching assistant) training or mentoring—as well as "pure" research and pedagogical preferences. If you have experience that prepares you for the job, but doesn't easily fit the *vita* format, the application letter can draw attention to it and demonstrate how it strengthens your other areas of expertise. The application letter is also the place to request accommodations such as a translator or wheelchair access.

Remember that search committees read a plethora of applications for each position. While they need to hear that you taught seventeen sections of composition emphasizing writing-across-the-curriculum, they want to hear what makes you different from all the other applicants with the same experience. What innovative ways did you use to promote classroom interdisciplinarity? Did you gain experience with computer-assisted instruction or with "at-risk" students while you were teaching those seventeen sections? Did you have (or make) the opportunity to create lesson plans or syllabi, choose texts, or set up the evaluation system in any of these courses? This is the place to show how you invested the standardized activities expected of all graduate students with your own personal flair. A word of caution, however: At least two department chairs we surveyed considered long-winded letters (more than two pages) an indication of hubris.

Let's look at a teaching-oriented, humanities-focused application letter of one of the authors, which helped win her a job at her first choice—a teaching-oriented institution that appreciates research. Identifying elements have been slightly changed:

November 25, 199–

Dr. V.I. Purson, Chair
Department of English
State College
City, State Zip

Dear Dr. Purson:

Enclosed is my application for the generalist position in English at State College. As you will note from the attached *vita*, I have focused my teaching, conference presentations, and publications on composition studies while integrating both literary and composition theories into my dissertation research. While I am thus equipped to teach both literature and composition, I prefer teaching composition. I like to challenge students to find issues that are important to them, and then guide them to invention, organization, and revision strategies that will help them develop their ideas.

Three years of graduate teaching at the University of Quixote grounded me in the theory and application of literature, composition, and liberal arts pedagogies. While completing coursework in nineteenth-century literature and in writing, I led discussions, graded papers, and guest lectured in literature classes and taught the writing component of a six-quarter, interdisciplinary humanities core sequence. As Senior Teaching Assistant with the Quixotic Writing Program, I gained administrative experience serving on the committee that trained new writing instructors, revised the instructor's manual, and helped TAs negotiate the inevitable pitfalls of teaching for lecturers from different disciplines.

A particularly satisfying graduate accomplishment was restrategizing a very demanding research project (creating an advertising campaign) for students in the Writing Program. By constructing "real-world" target audiences for our projects, my students and I were able to frame our research within the parameters of distinct language communities. Rather than feeling daunted by the project's requirements, several of my students won community awards for their work, were offered actual commercial space for their proposed displays, or saw their work "showcased" by the Writing Program. I presented these success stories at the State Council of Writing Programs, shared my teaching strategies with the following year's incoming TAs, and later adapted the assignment as a service-learning project in a community college setting. *Composing Ourselves* recently published my article describing how the "ads project" could be taught in different institutional settings.

My dissertation (defended in March, 199-) analyzes how popular narratives colluded with and contested the discourses of late nineteenth-century science and technology. The "spirited" debate over the existence of ghosts pit accounts of compelling subjective experience against disparate methods of defining, collecting, ranking, and interpreting evidence, reflecting larger epistemological dissensions within emerging disciplines. This research reflects my teaching interests in writing and language communities, science and culture, and nineteenth-century British culture.

While writing my dissertation, I went in search of students who were struggling academically or financially to stay in college. As a result, for the past two and a half years I have been teaching students from diverse cultural, economic, and ethnic backgrounds at a local community college. Where my graduate teaching grounded me in theory and pedagogy, my adjunct position in the community college has enabled me to invent various teaching strategies and course syllabi. One class I have developed asks students to think critically about their own negotiations of our increasingly technology-oriented culture. Offered as a "theme" class within Local College's selection of required first-year composition classes, the course presents scholarly research and critical thinking as directed analyses of popular science, technology, and culture. Although class assignments can be rigorous for the many students who hold full-time jobs as well as attend college, my students respond with enthusiasm. In fact, one of them delightedly reported that he'd been offered a job at a computer company while conducting field interviews for a class assignment.

In short, I am a teaching-oriented generalist whose intellectual interests reach back to nineteenth-century culture and forward to technologically enriched composition and communication. My teaching stresses critical analysis, clear communication, and effective presentation of ideas. My overall aim in dealing with students at every level is to construct an atmosphere of deep mutual respect and responsive, proactive problem solving. I am particularly drawn to students who think they "hate English."

I will be available for interviews at the upcoming MLA conference from Friday, December 27 through the morning of Monday, December 30. I would very much like to meet with you.

Sincerely,

Cheryl Reed
Address
Phone number
E-mail address

Now let's look at how this letter interprets, rather than regurgitates, *vita* information:

- Paragraph 1 clearly identifies which position Cheryl is applying for and sets up a framework within which to interpret the contents of the entire application packet: although the applicant has trained in several areas, she prefers teaching a field many applicants regard as a necessary duty. (Note: if you say something like this, be prepared to back it up with reasons why you feel that way. Cheryl was asked to elaborate on "I prefer teaching composition" in *every* interview she had.)

- Paragraph 2 directly relates graduate training to experience potentially valuable to the hiring institution. It specifies activities that reflect Cheryl's main focus—teaching—and specifically notes related activities on the administrative side of the bench.

- Paragraph 3 relates a project only this candidate could talk about. It gives an impression of teaching style (again, a main focus of this applicant's search).

- Paragraph 4 gives the obligatory description of the candidate's dissertation research. For an application to a very research-oriented institution, this discussion should be lengthened, deepened, and foregrounded. Any publications arising out of the dissertation research could also be noted.

- Paragraph 5 turns from graduate school experience to note the candidate's experience and teaching style with a student population other than that of her degree-granting university, highlighting the autonomy and professional experience this position allowed her as well as her engagement with very different student populations.

- Paragraph 6 offers a "sound bite" that sums up the applicant's message to reviewers. "Teaching-oriented generalist" would fit neatly on the scribbled list most search committee members make as they read stacks and stacks of applications.

- Paragraph 7 states the candidate's intention to pursue the position actively (this is no dry run; the candidate is spending money to go to her annual disciplinary conference to meet the search committee) and gives specific details about when and where she can be contacted. While this sounds like the driest portion of the letter, those 2-3 final lines are the last thing a reviewer reads and should act as a strong statement of your interest. Note: while these lines should radiate confidence, be careful not to perform an academic version of a used car ad: "This is your lucky day! Call now!"

We've offered an actual letter here instead of a sample because the application letter should be the most personal and vibrant part of an application packet. Unfortunately, as Virginia Carroll points out, "many of these letters sound the same, as if they were copied from books or written according to a formula." A well-crafted letter expresses your own voice. Candidates in the sciences, for instance, will want to show off their skills at summarizing key points (as one of our colleagues told us). Their application letters will thus be much shorter than our model letter—a *tour de force* of concise, scientific presentation (See appendix 4 for a sample science cover letter and *vita*.) Consider this excerpt from the application letter of an assistant professor in the humanities at a large East Coast college:

> My master's degree in criminology and professional experience in major and minor league baseball not only gave me an opportunity to develop the detail-oriented, decision-making side of my personality but also left me with a unique perspective on the importance of writing across disciplines and in the work-world. I would aim to develop a strong connection

between academic and professional writing realms, perhaps through a professional writing internship for Valley College students. I would also be interested in developing a collaborative, preparatory program between Valley College and area high schools to orient prospective college students to the rigors of academic writing and thinking. My roots in the Valley County business community would foster these developments.

Reviewers swamped in a Garrison Keiler-style search "(State U, where all our applicants are strong, attractive, and above-average!)" will certainly remember this candidate's letter.

How to Get Recommendation Letters that Work

As elementary as it may seem, many applicants don't discuss their work with their recommenders before they request letters for their application packets. Letters that result from such anonymous requests are most often vague and non-committal. A more productive strategy is to ask potential recommenders how they feel about your work and employability well in advance of application deadlines. If you get a positive response, give the recommender a copy of your *vita* and a sample application letter outlining your interpretation of your strengths as a candidate. Schedule a brief chat (again, well in advance of application deadlines) to discuss your work in light of available jobs and your own aspirations. Many recommenders appreciate your pointing out specific projects or areas on which you would like them to focus. One contributor reports that she gave the members of her dissertation committee "polished copies of chapters, papers, and even exams I had written." To those who'd agreed to write a teaching recommendation, she gave copies of student evaluations she'd received when she taught in their classes.

If this sort of relationship with mentors makes you uncomfortable, consider again that the job search marks your transition from graduate student to junior faculty member. This involves a parallel change in your relationship to mentors. In many cases, you will in fact be educating your committee members about the realities of the current academic job market.

One Visiting Assistant Professor writes:

It is absolutely essential that you know what your letters of recommendation say about you . . . I have had several unfortunate experiences regarding letters. One was a typographical error that caused a great deal of confusion for readers; in another letter, a well-meaning colleague discussed my achievements in light of the fact that I am a single mother. This personal information did not belong in a professional letter and may have caused some would-be employers to think of me as less capable than another candidate. Once you discover problems like these, you can tactfully ask your reference to rewrite the letter (check the rewrite, too!) or you can pull the letter from your file.

Many candidates suggest that kindred spirits in another educational institution send for your dossier and give it a quick check on potential bugs. That way, your file stays confidential, but you know if it contains any potential snafus.

Many career centers that house and distribute dossiers will do this sort of "blind read" on request. They will not compromise the confidentiality of the letters under their care, but they can rate individual letters in terms of strength and weight. The candidate can then choose which ones to include or exclude from each mailing. One contributor asked her school's director of graduate studies to read her letters of recommendation before they were mailed to schools where she was applying for jobs, while Casie Hermansson plied the dossier staff with questions: "what kind of documents others generally had on file, how many letters were sent out per application on average, costs, time frame for processing, and so on."

In addition to the traditional letters from members of your committee, try to obtain substantive letters from sources outside your institution. If you've worked in a two-year college, or participated in a community literacy project, or helped compile a bibliography related to your discipline, consider including recommendation letters from those who supervised your work. The letters that are most informative for your potential interviewers will come from sources inside and outside your institution, who know disparate aspects of your work well, and who are willing to promote your candidacy enthusiastically and knowledgeably. Ideally, this pool extends beyond your committee members.

In fact, one of the authors was told that her "outside" letters (one from a journal editor and another from a department chair in the community college where she adjuncted) weighed more heavily in her successful search than the standard, glowing letter generated by a member of her dissertation committee. Dissertation advisers, the thinking went, could be *expected* to praise their own work (the successful student), but "outsiders" were more likely to give a straightforward account of the candidate's work. Much the same thinking is expressed in tenure-track reviews that require work to be assessed by scholars in the discipline at large as well as by local colleagues.

How to Organize Application Records

Every graduate student on the job market has a favorite method of keeping track of application materials. The important thing is that you do keep track. If you're only applying to one or two positions, this doesn't take much effort. However, if you're like most people engaged in a faculty job search today, you'll send out far more than one or two applications.

Academic lore has long suggested that applicants include a stamped, self-addressed postcard with your application packet. Type a short message on the back of the card that gives the name of the university and a space to indicate your materials have been received:

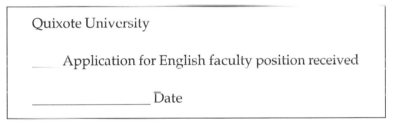

```
Quixote University

___  Application for English faculty position received

_____ Date
```

Since the volume of applications is so high, it's not good etiquette (and won't be taken seriously) to ask the person handling the mail to go back to your application more than once—for example, to tell you when your packet *and* your recommendation letters arrive. The card tells you that at least the materials you sent didn't get lost in the mail, as one of our contributors' materials for graduate art school did. Many schools have instituted their own postcard system: they'll send you a checklist of materials received so you can check up on anything that's missing. This is particularly important if something outside your direct control doesn't make it to the institution when you think it should. You can then ask your dossier service or your recommenders to check on letters—not because you're being a nuisance, but because a university with an opening has asked you to do so.

If you craft each application packet to the particular position for which you're applying, you'll need to keep track of what you said, when, and to whom. The easiest way to do this is to print out an extra copy of each job letter as you assemble the packet and keep it along with a copy of the job announcement. A simple three-ring binder with alphabetic dividers works well here. Job announcements can be cut and pasted or copied onto standard-size paper and filed alphabetically by state name (since many institutions start with "University of . . . ," filing alphabetically by name of institution tends to clog your "U" section). Add your copy of the application letter, along with notes about other materials you sent, the date these were sent, the specific recommendation letters you requested be sent, and the date you requested your campus dossier service to send them. When you get the self-addressed postcard back, or receive any sort of communication from one of the places to which you've applied, it's fairly simple to make a note on your file materials or staple any new correspondence to your original records.

If you are applying to several universities that have drastically different deadlines and timelines for their searches, you might consider adding a set of dividers that sorts by date, as well. Move "hot" materials—jobs you really hope to get a call on, or that do express preliminary interest in your application—from the generic, alphabetized section to the "dated" section, and file them under the month in which all materials must be received. This helps you get a feel for just how late in the search it is for any particular application. One contributor, for example, applied to a school that interviewed at the disciplinary conference in December, but continued to accept applications until late January. This put that search in a much different time frame than others that proceeded immediately to campus visits after the conference interviews. If your "ideal" opening is very much out of synch with other search schedules, the rough timetable you set up in your binder can help you gauge how to respond to offers from second- or third-choice institutions. You want to have a feel for how realistic your hope may be that your first choice will respond miraculously, just before you have to make a decision about another offer.

Keeping a record of what you sent to various openings will also help you avoid the embarrassing predicament of not remembering what you told a particular search committee. Questions like, "Tell us about that research project you did in San Diego!" (as Cheryl was asked by one dean) can be confusing if you've just spent the last five years in San Diego generating research. Several of our contributors, in fact, reported talking about unrelated projects when pitched that sort of question during interviews.

Summary

- Make sure your *vita* and application letter indicate clearly how your specialization and experience fit the job description. Addenda and qualifiers can be added after you've established your eligibility for the position.

- Take care to make pre-printed application forms neat, accurate, and readily intelligible to sorters outside your discipline.

- Arrange your application materials in logical, easy-to-read blocks of information. Make each document work for you: redundancy wastes space you could use to demonstrate your compatibility with the institution and the position.

- Clarify your terms and the terms of the position announcement. "I have finished my coursework and am presently completing my dissertation" or "I have taught composition to non-native writers for the past three years."

- Go beyond simply recounting your present job description in order to show your individual, one-of-a-kind contributions to each position listed in your c.v.

2

THE CALLBACK
The Professional Conference Interview

The First-Stage Interview as a Rhetorical Scene

The first-stage interview is actually the second phase of the application-to-contract process. Its format varies depending on the configuration of the institution to which you're applying. The traditional teaching or research-oriented university will most likely hold preliminary interviews at the disciplinary conference (attended at the candidates' expense). Community colleges, on the other hand, may invite twenty to twenty-five candidates to campus (again, at the candidates' expense), thus collapsing the tasks of this chapter and the next into one visit. Some (but not all) institutions do phone interviews rather than conference interviews for science positions. Despite some differences in form and content, however, both sets of institutions use the first-stage interview to continue the sorting begun when applications were distributed to search committee members.

If you receive a telephone call or letter requesting an interview at your discipline's conference (or a telephone interview, in some cases), you have survived the first cut. You have been selected from a group of 300 to 800 applicants. You are now likely part of a group of fifteen to twenty applicants who have been selected for a conference, community college campus, or telephone interview. Congratulations! Your paper persona has impressed the interviewers. Now your task is, as one search committee member told us, to narrate your credentials, to present yourself as the main character of the script that's being reviewed "on spec." (Later, during the on-campus interview, your task will be to campaign actively for the "votes" of individuals. In the community college interview, of course, you'll be narrating and campaigning simultaneously.)

Know that the application-to-contract process is a fully dimensional rhetorical scene. Rhetoric guides the dynamic processes of making meaning—even in interviews. Every act of communication involves a set of interrelationships among the sender, receiver, message, and context. Together these four components create meaning (Lunsford and Glenn 394). Within each communication moment, the sender and receiver repeatedly change roles both as they respond to specific messages and as they work together to create particular meanings.

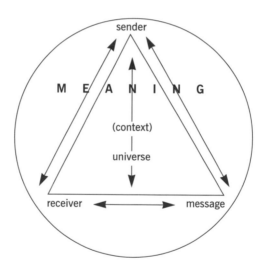

It is this dynamic communication triangle that alerts us to the language behaviors triggered by the very structure of interview questions and responses. The interview is a script undergoing continuous revision, one that has to be negotiated with some degree of humor and savvy. It's a reel in motion, a narrative being enacted by many individuals, a set that applicants need to assess from the moment the director says, "So, tell me about your dissertation."

The professional-conference, telephone, or community-college-campus first-stage interview puts the communication triangle illustrated above into practice. Up to this point, both you and the interviewing college or university have met each other on paper only. The interviewers have come to know you through your application letter, *vita*, letters of recommendation, and perhaps writing samples. You have come to know the respective interviewers through their college and university catalogs and web pages. Both you and the interviewers have developed interview questions for this first-stage interview based on these pre-established paper personalities. You and the interviewers want to use this brief first-stage interview, a meeting that typically lasts anywhere between twenty minutes (conference or telephone) to a full day (community college campus), to bring your paper personalities to life. Both you and the interviewees will be sending and receiving messages from each other in a particular academic context throughout the day(s). Recall that the sender, receiver, message, and context together create meaning. Most importantly, note the double-sided arrows in the communication triangle. These arrows should remind you that even at the interview you are never just the sender or receiver of messages. You and the interviewers send and receive messages throughout the interview, messages that you will come to understand more thoroughly as the interview progresses.

This first-stage interview has a tacit two-point agenda: 1) You and your interviewers want to know how your intellectual, teaching, service skills, and, for some scientists and medical applicants, licensure will complement the potential college or university; and 2) you want to gauge how pleasing you would find the work environment they describe. Although, as we mentioned earlier, it is not wise to approach your interviewers arrogantly or with grandiose assertions of your desirability as a candidate for the job under consideration, you at the same time should not feel at all obsequious. Rather, you want to approach the interview scene as a "dialogic"—a negotiated conversation with valued colleagues. You have the skills to prepare yourself for this mindset; your challenge is to recognize the experience and knowledge you already have.

Preparing for the Interview

RECOGNIZING WHAT YOU KNOW ABOUT HIGHER EDUCATION

To create the "dialogic," the negotiated conversation, recall your extensive experience in the academy. You are not green to the academy or to research, but you may be green to thinking about yourself as valuable part of the intellectual community. You know the scene well. You know what it means to be an academic today and what it means to prepare for academe's future:

- As a students you have benefited from the academy's increased use of technology. You have experienced new ways of learning and thinking as these technologies have provided new pedagogies.

- You have joined conversations about disciplinary debates and know where your ideas situate you.

- You can speak to the innovative pedagogical tools that are moving the academy into the twenty-first century.

- You know the benefits and challenges of open admissions policies, student populations whose varied needs and educational backgrounds add valuable dimensions to the classroom but also require a wide range of teaching strategies and close advising and counseling relationships to succeed.

- You continue to see what it means for colleges to undertake "self-governance" or corporate models of operation. You have experienced the workload effects of the academy's move towards corporate structures. You understand faculty workload issues from the perspective of a student, graduate assistant, or adjunct instructor.

Knowing the academy from your graduate student or adjunct positions can help you imagine yourself as a possible colleague, understand what your interviewers experience in their workaday lives, and relate to them as multidimensional, complex participants in a complex social context, rather than as stick figures with all the authority to keep you out of your profession of choice. Your experience in this newer academy authorizes you to speak about it as a participant, an insider. You already possess knowledge and experience of the academy; now you are poised on the threshold of professionalizing your position through being hired at a specific institution.

Your personal challenge before you begin the interviewing process is to remind yourself that you know all of this. It is not so much the case that you will engage conversations connected to all of the topics above; rather, by thinking about these topics, it will be easier for you to recognize that the interview process is a series of conversations where you are "rehearsing" your academic capital—your intellect, skill, and experience. Thus, your self-reflection on your knowledge of higher education should be an important part of preparing for the interview: It puts you in the mindset you need to fully operationalize the interview process.

THE MOCK INTERVIEW

Take advantage of the mock interviews, if you can. A practice interview is the best thing you can do to prepare. Really!
—*Assistant Professor*

As we've seen, recognizing your knowledge will allow you to present yourself as the composed candidate who thinks well on his or her feet. In addition, practicing the give and take of the interview beforehand will help you promote a "dialogic" interview—a negotiation of exciting ideas—rather than the "dialectic" contest most candidates expect from the interview experience. Since you're already well familiar with contesting ideas in the graduate seminar, your first task in mock interviews is experimenting with the ways in which you situate yourself in disciplinary debates. Where do you live and thrive, intellectually and personally, among the inevitable, rich diversity of theories swirling about your discipline? The "cutting edge" is not necessarily a bad place to be if you're aware what living there means, and how to talk to someone who, for instance, thinks your love affair with technology hooks you to a passing fad, or your passion for service learning is laudable, but misguided.

In your mock interviews, then, you will want to think about how you might respond to potential colleagues who wonder about your pedagogies, your theoretical stances, and your professional affiliations (see chapter 4 for practice interview scenarios that address these and other "sticky" situations). Stock responses, of course, are out, because they shut down communication rather than opening up a healthy exchange of ideas. If you present yourself as a negotiator rather than a contestor of such issues, you may even find that your interviewers were hoping for a valuable exchange of "cutting edge" information all along. Visiting Assistant Professor of English Jeanne-Marie Zeck shares her experience:

At one interview, someone asked me a question about how effective I'd been in teaching through distance-learning technology. I said, "I've never done it. Could you tell me how it works?" Surprisingly, looks of distress crossed several faces as the interviewers admitted they had never used the technology themselves.

An interview moment like this allows the candidate and interviewers to discuss honestly how such pedagogy could be launched at the campus. Your truthful, audience-specific responses will show that you are able to participate in the interview as a conversation, not as a halting thrust and parry, "dialectic" session.

Unfortunately, many universities fail to provide mock interviews fortheir graduating Ph.D.'s. Thus, the practice interview many candidates experience is their less-than-stellar conference or campus encounter with the institution that's first on their interview schedule. While this may work if you have several interviews and the most desirable ones are scheduled last, it's more productive to orchestrate your own mock interview. If your institution doesn't offer practice interviews as a matter of course, someone interested in your success may be willing to stage a mock interview for you, alone, even if such preparation isn't standard procedure. Again, do this early in the application process. While you may feel foolish asking for help before you've received any callbacks, nevertheless prepare as if you will be interviewed. Requests for interviews can come as late as the day before an interview is to occur—too late to set up the necessary practice session. Whether or not your training institution provides such help with your job search, you can prepare yourself for tough interview questions before you face an interview in real-time. If your Ph.D.-granting institution doesn't offer these helpful mock interviews, you may consider creating your own mock interviews with the help of your graduate student peers and of recently employed graduates of your program.

We encourage you to practice both conference and telephone interviews. You may even choose to organize a job clinic for you and your peers, as Casie Hermansson and Margaret McGeachy did when they were graduate students. Hermansson explains,

> We conceived of an all-day seminar for graduate students in English on the academic job search to be followed by a hands-on documents workshop. It is important to consider our resources: as graduate students we are already well-trained in techniques for approaching the job search. Getting information and sharing it is what we do. [See appendix 3 for a full description of this workshop.]

We promise you that whether you take advantage of your program's organized mock interviews or create your own mock interviews with your graduate student peers, the practice will benefit you.

RESEARCHING THE SCHOOLS BEFORE YOUR INTERVIEW

> I am always more impressed with candidates who have done their homework—those who are familiar with the schools at which they are interviewing. Researching the schools is time well-spent.
> —*Regina Eisenbach, Associate Professor of Management*

In addition to thinking through and practicing your professional self-presentation, do research on the institution(s) with which you hope to interview. Familiarize yourself with university-wide programs and departmental courses via university catalogues, recruitment pamphlets and administrative websites. This information will help you prepare school-specific questions. Well-directed questions will help you stand out as a prepared faculty candidate. Research into the interviewing institution will also help you anticipate potential questions. Associate Professor of English Virginia Carroll advises,

> Find out what you can about the institution and department: with the abundance of institutional, departmental, and individual web pages, candidates can easily find out about the places to which they are applying. By referring to specific courses within a curriculum or institutional mission, candidates demonstrate that they are willing to look beyond their own field of specialty to see how their contributions would fit into the larger picture of a department or campus.

Another contributor adds that she found some search committee members who graduated from her degree-granting institution:

> I look at their dissertations for any useful bibliographical information about them, their academic interests, and theoretical perspectives. This information proved useful for fielding questions from these particular faculty members during interviews.

As schools contact you requesting dossiers and writing samples, start researching. If a school expresses interest in you, begin to familiarize yourself with their program and faculty. When the support staff or search committee member contacts you to schedule the interview, you may ask who is on the committee. Knowing the committee members' names will help you anticipate more fully the search committee audience. Once you have search committee members' names, you can research their respective areas of expertise and anticipate particular questions. For instance, if you are a sociologist who works primarily with qualitative research and one of your interviewers is a quantitative guru, you can certainly anticipate a question about the relationship in your research between both types of data. You want to know what your interviewers' research areas are, and you want to note their key publications (this is especially true for research universities). You also want to familiarize yourself with each school's catalog (this is especially true for community college positions):

- What does the university's mission statement emphasize?
- Are there student services and resources that intersect with your teaching, research, and community service interests?
- Do you recognize faculty members' names? Do your advisors recognize faculty names at the prospective campus?
- Are there interdepartmental programs in which you would imagine participating?

Such background research, then, should help you craft thoughtful questions to ask of the search committee. As Virginia Carroll points out, the information which your interview questions request should not be easily accessible in the catalog or website. Your interview is not a "confirmation hearing" of what you read in the catalog, but rather a chance to expand on the things you learned there. As you're surfing these electronic resources, remember that— just as your web page is a public declaration of who you are—the departmental website is the public face of the institution. One search committee member reminded us that departmental websites are more likely to "sell" electives and other perks than the service courses which are the bread and butter of most institutions.

   If you are sending out multiple applications and anticipate several first-stage interviews, you certainly won't have time to conduct in-depth background research for every potential school. We suggest that you conduct this search committee research only as you receive clear signs (a phone call or letter that says "Look for our university at the conference") or confirmation that you will be interviewed. Conducting this research on an "as contacted" basis will make the days and nights just before the conference interviews more sane.

Although the application-to-contract process takes seven to nine months, a seemingly long time, there are serious spurts of craziness. The time just before the conference interview is one of those periods. (Community college application deadlines, on the other hand, spring up at unpredictable times, as positions and funding emerge. This is crazy-making in its persistent regenerations of application-making.) Despite this time crunch, however, pre-interview research is time well spent, even if you are simultaneously finishing writing your dissertation.

QUESTIONS TO EXPECT AT THE CONFERENCE INTERVIEW

"So tell me about your dissertation." You should expect this request at your conference, community college, and university on-campus interviews. After spending years preparing to write your dissertation and after spending months (sometimes years) writing it, you are the expert. You have specialized knowledge about your topic. You can speak about this topic at great length and in some depth. However, in interviews, you'll be forced to explain your ideas in a five-minute sound bite that interests a group of academics who typically do not share your specialization. The "so tell me about your dissertation" question is more accurately a genre of interview questions and is one of the three most common conference interview questions. The Search Committee, however, may phrase the question in a variety of ways. To prepare for the dissertation-genre question, anticipate questions such as these:

- What does your dissertation title mean?
- I recognize your dissertation chair. In what ways does her scholarship inform your dissertation?
- Why did you write the dissertation you did?
- How did you come to your dissertation topic?
- How does your research inform your teaching?
- How does your teaching inform your research?

While some of the above questions are more likely to be asked at the conference interview for a university than the campus interview for the community college, all candidates should anticipate at least one other question:

• What kinds of courses can you bring to our campus?

The questions asked at the first-stage interview are revealing. Listen for those questions, especially if you are interested to know how particular institutions value teaching and research. Be careful not to assume that teaching schools won't value research or that research institutes won't value teaching. As an associate professor who would like to remain anonymous told us,

> In my graduate school all of the faculty were really pushing us towards Ph.D. granting institutions and research. We were spending our lives doing research. That was all that was encouraged. What I found on the market was a search for generalists: people who could fill a lot of university gaps and goals.

More schools across the board are interested in candidates who show skill across the three major areas of professional evaluation: teaching, research, and community service. Community colleges will want to know how being at a teaching-oriented institution with a heavy service component reconciles with your obvious pleasure in and adeptness for research (see our discussion on community college interview *foci* in chapter 6.)

Questions about what courses you can teach provide real opportunities for you to show your interview preparedness. In sketching out briefly the kinds of classes you would bring to the school, you may be able to speak to the way you would offer a writing-intensive version of the course or a version that focuses on the topic through a multicultural or gendered lens. By suggesting these different ways of teaching a particular class, you show not only your range and flexibility as an instructor but also your awareness of the curriculum issues that are unique to particular campuses. After researching the school, you may also be aware of interdisciplinary teaching opportunities, so you may suggest working with a colleague from another discipline in your college or in another college such as business or education to team-teach and cross-list a class. The school may also have special programs such as gender or ethnic studies that do not exist as departments but instead as programs that rely on faculty from around the college. You will want to show how your teaching interests may complement those programs.

As you anticipate the interviewers' questions, imagine their questions as an opportunity to showcase your creative contributions to your field. Talking about the following kinds of professional contributions will help your interviewers see who you are as a future colleague:

- projects you've initiated,
- difficult situations you've encountered and how you coped with them,
- or why you want to work for a particular university (subjects well-trod in the business-oriented interview guides listed in our appendix 5).

Making these kinds of comments will help them understand the skillful ways your teaching, research, and community service intersect. They want to hear those connections. Should you agree to an offer from them, your colleagues will want you to succeed. They will want you to earn tenure at their institution. Thus, the more convinced they are that you understand the range of your professional responsibilities and that you bring creative problem solving skills to their program, the more likely it is that you will receive an offer from that school.

To prepare for additional interview questions, we encourage you to turn to books in the job-guide genre. While the academic press is strangely silent on this front, the business world is awash with guides for interview preparation (see appendices 1 and 5 for websites and some suggestions of recent publications in this genre). Some of the best publications along these lines are guides such as Medley's *Sweaty Palms* (1992) or Jeff Allen's *Complete Question and Answer Job Interview Book* (1988). Books like these list literally hundreds of frequently asked and/or tricky questions that need only a bit of tweaking in order to foreshadow an academic interview (see chapter 4 for a list of business interview questions "tweaked" to reflect the academic interview).

PREPARING QUESTIONS TO ASK OF THE SEARCH COMMITTEES

As you prepare for the first-stage interview, don't neglect to prepare questions to ask of the search committee. Job counselor Jeff Allen tells his clients that communication in an interview flows both ways. (Recall the communication triangle). You interview the prospective colleagues represented by the search committee as much as they are interviewing you. Assistant Professor of Psychology Gina Grimshaw adds that part of the interview process is candidates asking questions of the committee. The committee wants to know what's on the candidate's mind. Such advice reminds us as the Lunsford and Glenn communication triangle illustrates, you are never just a sender or receiver of information. In an interview you want to consciously send and receive information (messages). Recalling the intersection of the sender and receiver sides of the communication triangle will help you to avoid collapsing the triangle into a single line that runs from interviewer to applicant alone.

Prepare specific questions for the interviewers about the department and the university such as these:

- What is the relationship between specific disciplinary subdivisions in your department?

- What role does the department play in other university programs?

- How would you describe the theory that informs your department?

Your questions are your opportunity to do your preliminary screening of a particular school: you are reading their narrated script. You certainly don't want to monopolize the conference interview with your questions; you want the participants in the communication triangle to share the talking and listening opportunities. Remember, as Assistant Professor of Economics Ranjeeta Ghiara told us, "Usually new applicants are very tentative. More experienced colleagues ask questions."

The first-stage or community college campus interview is also the time to find out about the configuration of the student population, community attitudes toward the hiring institution, computer access for faculty and students, and other issues you think will directly affect your decision to continue pursuing the position. You can gather that information by asking questions like:

- My teaching experience at the community college convinced me that I really enjoyed working with returning students. In reviewing your catalog, I noticed several degree programs designed specifically for returning students. Can you tell me about the various student populations on your campus?

- I realize that I am asking for an unfair generalization of sorts, but how would you describe the range of students in your department's 100-level courses? 300-level courses? How do the range of students work together in your classes?

- In reviewing your catalog, I noticed that your department is directly involved in providing outreach programs for skill development at the feeder high schools. How does the non-academic community or the town feel about the program?

- Your department's web page caught my attention. How would you describe student and faculty access to technology at your institution?

Notice that each of these information-gathering questions reveals your knowledge of the campus while also complimenting the institution. Phrasing questions in this way is smart rhetorically. You want to invite the interviewers to say as much as they can about the department's politics, the student population, or computer access issues. You want the interviewers to initiate conversations about potential university, college, or departmental weaknesses. Your job is to listen for those rhetorical clues. Does it appear that the interviewers are not wanting to reveal information that you really do need to know? Make a mental note of that (when you finish the interview jot those observations down in your notes). The interview, of course, is not the place to challenge the interviewers about a rhetorical snag that you notice. At the first-stage interview, you want to gather information. You will not impress your interviewers by engaging in the dialectic for which you have been so well trained. Interviewers generally don't want that training used on them.

Going to the Interview

WHAT TO BRING TO THE ACTUAL INTERVIEW

As the candidate, you want to imagine the interview as a Burkean parlor. In other words, you want to approach the interview as a conversation in which you and the interviewers create a collaborative understanding of the professional relationship that might result from the interview. You want to walk in prepared to have a smart conversation, not prepared to give a thesis defense. You, instead, want to present yourself as a future colleague who is joining the Search Committee for a conversation.

That means you will likely bring materials with you—carried rather discretely in your attaché. Bring extra copies of your *vita* and writing sample. You should also prepare working bibliographies or syllabi for at least two courses you would be interested in teaching at that particular institution. Watch the pacing of the conversation to see when to introduce these materials (if at all). Obviously, you devoted much time to preparing these materials, but you don't want to foist them on unwilling recipients. Instead, by keeping these materials in your bag, when and if the appropriate moment arises in the conversation, you can say, "Oh, yes! I am very interested in your program's canonical/creative curriculum. In fact, I have ideas about how I would teach your program's 403 class. Let me show you what I have thought about that" (pull out the syllabi for discussion). Or, if an interviewer appears to be fumbling for a copy of your *vita* as (s)he wades through twenty other *vitae* in the stack, you may offer to pull an extra copy out of your bag. (Conversely, if your interviewers can talk about key elements of your *vita* without even glancing back at it to refresh their memories, be impressed. Be very impressed.) As you pull these magical handouts from your bag, stay open to hearing how things are getting done without you at that particular institution, and, of course, how your actions make individual interviewers appear to their colleagues. Treat this as a discussion of options among colleagues, just as you would as a new colleague asked to share his or her ideas in a committee meeting. You want to invite your interviewers to imagine teaching the class, or working with you, in a particular way.

In preparing for our interviews, we found it useful to put together a file for each interview. We chose to create a simple set of files instead of collecting them all in a notebook simply because a file at a time is less cumbersome to pull out and review quickly before an interview than a clumsy three-ring notebook. You will find it useful to review your application letter before each interview, as it will remind you of the specifics of each job announcement and the questions you've jotted down to ask about a particular institution. As one of our contributors points out, the quick review will also keep you from seemingly contradicting what your application materials said.

The files we prepared for our interviews each included a copy of the application letter we sent, a list of the specific questions we prepared for each campus, a blank page for post-interview notes (for ourselves), and syllabi or writing samples (for our interviewers). These "debriefing" notes were a wonderful way to keep track of interviews. You'll find, in re-reading your post-interview notes, that you are pretty honest about how the interview went. These are useful notes to have as you prepare for the campus interview and as you negotiate contracts.

What and How to Pack for the Conference Interview

THE RHETORIC OF THE INTERVIEW SUIT

Now for what would seem to be the vainest of questions, what should you wear? This is not a stupid question, especially for female candidates. Unfortunately, audiences tend to be much more critical of what women wear than their male counterparts. Most of our advice in this section is thus for women, but male candidates take note: give some attention to the rhetoric of what you wear to the interview. What you wear contributes to the rhetorical scene, because your appearance suggests how you might fit into the campus community. One male candidate, for example, came to the interview in an ill-fitting suit, giving an overall impression of sloppiness.

Although you know the kind of clothes you wear as a candidate shouldn't really matter, if you are a woman, you may have received some of the common advice given to female candidates about "proper" dress. Most of it should be ignored:

- Women have been told quite candidly, "I know this is sexist, but dress like a man—but not to the extent of wearing pants."
- Others have also been told not to wear anything that fits feminine stereotypes: "Don't wear pastel—or brightly-colored suits."
- Still other women have been advised, "Don't wear jewelry that will distract you or your interviewers."
- Others have been coached about their body language: "Be sure not to fidget with your hair or clothes."

The tacit dress-code is not as firmly established as some mentors might have you believe. Women in pants and bright colors do get hired. All of this advice is well-meaning, but in our experience, the sagest advice is to be professionally comfortable, even if it means challenging the sexist advice you may receive.

Wear what feels right to you and fits the interview situation. You may find your interviewers dressed less formally than you. This doesn't mean you're over-dressed, or that your interviewers aren't taking their time with you seriously. It means that you packed for a series of professional interviews, while your interviewers packed for a more relaxed week of conference talks and discussions with colleagues. In sharing her interview experience, one faculty candidate told us,

> I was overdressed: silk suit, Bandolini suede high heels to match, silk shell, small gold hoop earrings and pendant. I was, after all, going to be interviewed by one of the major universities in this region. One of my women interviewers wore cotton twill slacks, a sweater, and loafers; another had on a blue chambray muu-muu and clogs. Even though I felt a bit out of costume, the interview was pleasant.

Clearly the candidate's dress set her apart from the interviewers and the interviewers each dressed distinctly (and comfortably). On the one hand, the range of styles hints at an eclectic campus. On the other hand, the candidate's and interviewers' dress don't seem to interrupt the real focus of the meeting: to have the candidate discuss her credentials. (Incidentally, this candidate later reported to us that she'd gotten the job.)

PACKING YOUR BAGS

While we don't intend to prescribe an interview dress-code for you, we found the conference interview to be a two-suit experience. Conferences tend to allow schools to conduct interviews throughout the three- to five-day conference. If you have scheduled several interviews over the course of a few days, you should not feel obligated to have a different interview suit for each day. Alternating a suit each day worked well for us. It also made packing a cinch. To keep the suits wrinkle-free and to ensure that you will not be stranded at the conference with only the clothes on your back, we encourage you to pack your interview materials and clothes in two bags: an attaché and a roll-on suitcase, one that fits in the airplane overhead bins. Let us also suggest that you pack earplanes brand ear plugs (marketed by Cirrus Air Technologies, L.L.C., P.O. Box 469, Locust Valley, New York, 11560, telephone 1-800-EAR-6151). These ingenious plugs help equalize the changing pressure in your ear canal as the plane changes altitudes. Inexpensive and relatively unobtrusive, earplanes greatly lessen the agony and temporary hearing loss experienced by fliers like Cheryl, who finds take-offs and descents prolonged forms of torture. Other fliers recommend using both lip balm to avoid chapped lips caused by the dry, artificial air of the pressurized cabin and Static Guard to eliminate static-y clothes and hair. Other contributors suggest that you not wear contact lenses on planes (red eyes are difficult to hide). To ensure that you arrive to interviews on time, pack a travel alarm clock. You may also want to pack portable snacks like protein bars or water for sustenance while running from interview to interview.

These simple suggestions will allow you to stay focused on your interviews so that you are not distracted by your clothes and your health. Consequently, you will project a very competent image.

The interview on the community college campus is generally a bit more relaxed (in the realm of dress, at any rate) than the conference interview. While a suit is still appropriate, you might choose to dress as if you were scheduled to teach that day (after all, you are.)

How to Negotiate the Logistics of the Professional Conference Interview

WHAT TO EXPECT OF THE CONFERENCE INTERVIEW SET(UP)

The conference interview is controlled chaos, even for those disciplines that typically schedule interviews with candidates well in advance of the conference. For those disciplines (such as business) that save the scheduling of interviews for the actual conference, the experience feels even more chaotic. Each conference has an interview check-in. At this checkpoint, a receptionist will confirm the location of the interview. We encourage you to find this check-in location the day before your interviews begin. You'll simply feel more comfortable getting to and from your interviews in the days ahead.

You will likely experience one of two (or maybe both) interview scenes at the disciplinary conference: serial interviews in a large room with other candidates looking, or very focused interviews with a group of Search Committee members in a less public setting. The more typical setting for conference interview is a large room filled with interview tables with numbers on each table. This scene alone can be stress-inducing as the room is filled with anticipatory candidates, and consequently feels like a great cattle call. (In fact, cynics in our discipline started calling this the "meat market," which conference organizers craftily transfigured into "meet market" in official flyers.) However, you may find yourself being interviewed in the quasi intimacy of an interviewer team's hotel room. (It is odd, and disconcerting to some candidates, to sit through an interview on the interviewer's bed, but the group format of hotel-room interviews lessens the strangeness of this scene quite a bit.)

LESSONS FROM THE GREAT ROOM

If your conference interview is in an oversized great room, the receptionist will tell you which table is yours. You simply approach the table when it is your interview time. If you notice that the interviewers are running a bit late, it is appropriate for you to approach the table to signal that you are ready but willing to wait. In the great room, the chairs are usually arranged so that the candidate is on one side of the table; and the interviewer(s) on the other side. If the Search Committee is large, together you will usually create a circle around the table. Search Committees usually try to make their interview space in the huge room as professionally intimate as possible.

Many candidates in the "meet market," however, are blatantly terrified: They hunch forward, as if to protect their vital organs, and tension creases their faces. One candidate waiting alongside Cheryl in the great room was so obviously nervous, in fact, that Cheryl walked over and whispered, "Smile! You're going to do just fine!" Minutes later, however, her fellow candidate was again hunched and frowning. Independent scholar Kass Fleisher tells a similar story:

> When I leave the hotel room I find waiting in the hall my interviewers' next appointment. My competitor. She looks so young. I walk up to her and extend my hand to shake. She stares at me like I am an alien. Her shake is noodle-limp. "They're very nice," I say. She stares at me in an uncomprehending fear, as if I have demanded her wallet.

The point to remember here is that your very presence in the interview hall means that one or more schools have found your application materials compelling. You are one of the successful handful of candidates that has already made the "first cut." Stand tall. Smile! Unlike the participants in the classroom dialectic, search committee members are not out to catch you in a mistake:

> "Aha! What you fail to account for is the bipolar panopticism inherent in your response!"

Rather, they want to find a new colleague to share their workload with as little disruption to their own workaday routines as possible. You do have what it takes. That's what got you this far. Show it.

LESSONS FROM THE BEDROOM

Most search committees admit that having to conduct formal interviews in hotel bedrooms can be awkward: you are being brought into someone's intimate space for a formal meeting. Committees who conduct meetings in bedrooms usually do so as a last resort. For whatever reason, they have not been able to secure a table in the great room or reserve a hotel suite. Since hotel rooms can, of course, be located any number of places around the conference city, it is especially important to locate the one in which you'll be interviewing as soon as you have that information, and to calculate any extra travel time you may need to get from the conference proceedings to your interview. When you arrive for the hotel room interview, you may also want to call from the hotel lobby to let the committee know that you are on your way. This phone call extends a thoughtful professional courtesy, allowing the Search Committee time to change from a "private" to a more "public" relational mode.

When you arrive at the room, take note of the arrangement of interview chairs. Is there room for everyone to sit in a chair? Is the room so small that you will be pinned against the wall with a row of chairs in front of you? Will you or the interviewers be resigned to sitting on the bed? As you notice the scene, quickly assess whether the arrangement is comfortable to you. You might be able to suggest another chair arrangement that would be more conducive to talking. If you would like to make such a suggestion, you might say something like, "I am concerned that as I respond to individual questions my back will be turned to some of you. What would you think of turning the chairs in this way?" Making your request in this way is usually welcomed. The interviewers generally want to make the interview as comfortable as possible for everyone.

Kass Fleisher relates her humorous experience with a Search Committee in the bedroom:

> "I'm, sorry, what was your question again?" The white man at the table has caught me staring at the man on the bed, who has just elaborately crossed his ankles and clasped his hands behind his head. Consequently, his suit jacket has flapped open and sprawls across the bedspread. It has a lovely silk lining. The chair speaks again from the bed, wagging his top foot back and forth as he speaks. The movement jiggles the entire bed.

Such an extremely relaxed hotel room setup can be distracting, but rest assured it's unusual. Thus, if you do find yourself in a hotel room with the search committee, don't read too much into the setup. Even Freud would say that sometimes a cigar is just a cigar, a bed just a place to sit. Some search committees, in fact, use the hotel room setting to make the interview more relaxed and personable than the noisy, angst-ridden atmosphere of the great room. Cheryl's interviewers, for instance, offered her fruit, cookies, and Perrier (two flavors). (Helpful hint: don't select potentially drippy fruit.)

Preparing for Telephone Interviews

Many candidates find telephone interviews (used by community colleges and increasingly by other types of institutions) to be the most awkward interviews they experience. You don't know who is talking and you can't see anyone. You don't realize how much you rely on body language to guide your conversation until you do a phone interview. Assistant Professor of English Robert D. Sturr recounts a scene from his telephone interview:

> On the phone I mis-heard a question. I thought they asked why I wanted to come to their campus when in fact they asked why they would want me. So, I started talking about my perspective. They quickly corrected me, and then I made some joke. That helped. In general, it was an unusual set up, but because I had decided early on that I wasn't going to see the job as something I desperately wanted, I didn't get flustered.

Time constraints because of long-distance costs are another element that can also affect the rhetoric of the telephone interview. One associate professor related a telephone interview in which she was told, "You have a minute and forty-five seconds to answer this question." While such comments can seem like stress tactics, rest assured that most interviewers are no more prepared to negotiate telephone interviews than they are face-to-face meetings. They are coping (at varying levels of distress) with the same peculiar elements of the voice-only exchange as you are: lack of visual clues, a heightened cognizance of time constraints, and socially awkward "dead time" (when no one speaks).

While these interviews can be strange, for some campuses they are a necessary step in the hiring process. In fact, one of our contributors from the sciences had never heard of candidates having face-to-face interviews at the preliminary stage. Schools may not have been able to reserve a table or a hotel room at the conference. The university or college may not have the resources to send the entire Search Committee to the conference. Telephone interviews happen for a range of reasons and are not unique to the conference interview. You may have a phone interview before the conference interview, or it may be a follow-up to the conference or campus interview. Virginia Carroll suggests that phone interviews may be on the rise. She told us,

> Although in the past, preliminary interviews may have been held *en masse* at professional conferences, many institutions are now using available technology to have such conversations in more efficient, economical ways. Few places have the capacity, at this point, for such interviews to have a video component, so the situation is very difficult for candidates.

You should expect that in the next few years, telephone and interactive television and computer interviews will be on the rise.

How awkwardly the telephone interview "plays" depends largely upon you. Cheryl—characteristically non-conformist—actively enjoyed her telephone interviews. She wore a disreputable old robe (which she now wears when she telephones publishers), sat on the floor, and scattered files, notes, and college catalogs all around her for easy reference. Pauses in conversation gave her time to consult or write additional notes, and the lack of visual cues was a real relief. The voice-only format of the telephone interview gave the fiction-writing portion of her brain a rest from constructing descriptive passages about the way an interviewer tilted his head, or smoothed and resmoothed her skirt. Further, no Socratic teaching muse emerged to make her ask a self-effacing interviewer, "You're frowning. Talk to me about what you don't understand." For once, she was able to concentrate only on the actual information being exchanged. Thinking it unreasonable to expect voice-only identifications of people she'd never met, she answered each question as it came and didn't worry about naming each speaker as multiple interviewers shared the line. Her one concession to the conference format of the call was to speak more loudly than is her custom. Yet, she was invited for a campus interview at more than one institution on the basis of such relaxed conversations.

Dawn, on the other hand, will laughingly tell you that she prepared for the telephone interview as she would for a face-to-face interaction. She awoke early, went over her notes, and dressed in her interview suit. Doing so simply put her in the "right" frame of mind. She began the interviews by introducing herself and (if necessary) requesting clarification of telephone interview etiquette:

> "So that I can be certain to answer each of your specific questions, would you mind telling me your name before each question?"

Most interviewers, however, made this request unnecessary. Typical question sequences in Dawn's telephone interviews went something like this:

> "Hi. It's Anne again. It is my turn to ask a question. Can you tell me what kinds of theoretical perspectives inform your dissertation?"

Dawn also found that her research about the Search Committee members helped minimize the awkwardness of voice-only communication. Since her preliminary research about the school and faculty familiarized her with the faculty members' names, she didn't find it necessary to ask for clarification of each interviewer's name. Seemingly inconsequential things like these made for a more pleasant interview experience. Dawn also received several invitations to campus visits as a result of her telephone interviews.

Construct the parameters of the telephone interview, then, according to your own relational style. Since you have more control over the physical parameters of the telephone interview than you do over any other type of interview scene, you can create the setting most conducive to a relaxed, confidence-making interchange. You will prepare for this interview much like you will for in-person interviews. The difference is the lack of non-verbal cues, including dress and body language. As we've seen, if you're hyperaware of these things in everyday interactions, avoiding them in this potentially stressful situation can actually be a plus. We encourage you to keep the following tips in mind:

- Create a comfortable place to sit during your interview. You will likely want to be seated in a quiet place where you can take notes. This might be an office desk, a kitchen counter, or a room with enough floor space to spread out your notes.

- Second, (as contributor Casie Hermansson suggests) obtain a telephone headset so that you can keep your hands free for writing, gesturing, and fidgeting.

- Third, although we discouraged you from taking notes during a conference interview, it is a great idea during the phone interview.

- Fourth, (as contributor Virginia Carroll recommends) practice the format. Carroll explains, " You talk on the phone all the time, and you may have even been through interviews. But interviewing on the phone is a new challenge, and practice would be a good idea. Anticipate questions and ask a friend or colleague to call you and interview you."

- Fifth, "Listen carefully to the questions," Carroll adds. "Candidates sometimes, out of nervousness or over-anticipation of the questions, answer what they think the committee asked instead of what it really asked. As much as possible, view this situation like a conversation."

- Finally, there is certainly no dress code for the phone interview. Like the conference interview, be sure you are comfortable. Unlike the conference interview, if that means jeans and a t-shirt (or a very old robe), perfect.

Summary

The conference, community college on-campus, and phone interviews, just like the application and university on-campus interview, represent rhetorical scenes. These interviews are moments for candidates and interviewers to construct meaning together about how well a prospective faculty candidate might fit into an existing department. They are not meant to be defenses of your training, experience, personal choices, or intellectual capabilities.

- Know that you are responsible for all expenses connected with the conference interview. You may be able to offset some of your travel expenses by presenting a paper or chairing a panel at the conference; if so, plan for this possibility well in advance. Some degree-granting institutions also agree to fund their new Ph.D.'s for one trip to the disciplinary conference for interviews. Check with your institution.

- Prepare for the conference, telephone, or community college on-campus interview by researching the school and faculty before the interview.

- Craft school-specific questions whose answers will help you determine how well you might fit in the program. Remember that the interview is an opportunity for you to be interviewed and to interview. Keeping this point in mind will help you present yourself as the well-composed candidate.

- Participate in at least one mock interview before you head to any sort of interview.

- Pack clothes that allow you to be professionally comfortable.

- Bring extra copies of your *vita* and writing sample. You will also want to develop sample syllabi for at least two courses, whether or not you decide to share these with interviewers.

- Keep a file for each school so that you can keep your specific questions and notes organized.

- Allow yourself a few minutes before each interview to review your school-specific questions, and allow yourself a few minutes after each interview to jot down the names of the search committee and your reactions to the interview.

- Prepare for the telephone interview the same way you would for face-to-face exchanges, but use your control of the setting to activate your self-confidence and enliven your self-presentation.

- If you're applying to community colleges, the interview events discussed in this chapter and chapter 3 will be happening simultaneously.

3

THE SCREEN TEST

The Campus Interview

To me some of the nitty gritty situations came as a surprise: I was expecting the highest levels of professionalism from everyone, as per the handbooks my mentors had recommended. But I certainly didn't meet with that, and I think job searchers should know what weirdness lurks out there.

—Assistant Professor

Here are the two most important things about interviewing: Show your enthusiasm and energy for teaching and always tell the truth.

—Visiting Assistant Professor of English Jeanne-Marie Zeck

The On-site Interview as a Rhetorical Scene

The on-campus interview adds travel arrangements, extended contact with interviewers, disparate interview tasks and audiences, and multiple sites to the considerations inherent in the conference interview. It builds on all of the rhetorical scenes you've negotiated to this point: your reading of the job announcement, your careful crafting of the application packet, and your successful participation in telephone and/or conference interviews. Since being interviewed on campus at the institution's expense and considerable time investment implies a deeper level of interest in your candidacy than does the conference "meet market," this interview also adds the pressure of making life-altering decisions to the mix. (For issues particular to the community college interview, see "The Tenure-Track Professorship at the Community College," chapter 6.) Not only will you be questioned by interviewers, and in turn question them, you will probably question yourself and your perceptions of the rhetorical scenes you encounter (see chapter 4 for practice interview scenarios). Yet—while the campus interview can be existential, it can also be epiphanic.

The campus interview is by far the most intensely interactive stage of the entire job search. You will be meeting with search committee members, other faculty members, staff, and administrators in both formal and informal contexts. These varied players will have made room in their always over-packed schedules to meet you and attend your presentation—even freeing up their students to have time with you—so the experience can be quite affirming and gratifying as well as crazy-making. This is your chance to meet these potential fans.

The on-campus interview is a time of many, many conversations, in varied modes, coming from disparate agendas, but all geared ultimately to assessing how your style, interests, and personal quirks fit an existing group complexly composed of many styles, many interests, and many more personal quirks. Although, of course, competence continues to be a key factor in the on-campus interview, it is much less the focus. The conference interviewers have already deemed you to have a high level of competence by the mere act of inviting you to come for further interviews. While you thus may receive some very specific questions about research interests or teaching practices from future colleagues who have not yet had the chance to talk to you, the underlying goal in all of this is to find the answers to the following questions:

- Will (s)he fit in with our campus, our students, our community, our location and resources?
- Will (s)he like it here?

And, the perennial question in every potential colleague's mind:

- How will this candidate lessen my workload?

Students will especially want to discern your attitude toward their particular group (returning students, different genders and ethnicities, members of a particular major, graduate students) and your ability to communicate your area of expertise in a way that's meaningful to them.

As you've probably already guessed, then, the main task of the on-campus interview is to show how you might inhabit the part that's been scripted and rehearsed in previous encounters. Think of it as a screen test or a dress rehearsal—a full-fledged run-through of an upcoming production for which you've run lines, crafted an interpretation of your character's motivation, and developed an intuitive sense of how your role might complement the roles of other players. In short, for the space of a few days, you will "try on" the role of a faculty member at a given institution. This is less a "star" performance aimed at some external audience of auditors than it is a "guest appearance" in which you participate in an ongoing production as a temporary member of an established troop of players. The more comfortable you are in the role of junior colleague, the more likely it is that your on-campus "screen test" will result in being offered "the part."

As we urged in the chapter on the applications packet (chapter 1), step confidently (but not arrogantly) into the professional persona you've imagined for yourself: function as that junior colleague you hope to become. Soak up the atmosphere of the campus community and the region that surrounds it. Talk to students (preferably without any other authority figures around to assess you or them) and pay attention to the implications of what they say about their school and community. If time alone with students is not scheduled for you, make your own. Get a Coke in the cafeteria; talk to students in the library or the commons area. In your meetings with future colleagues, be alert to personalities, collegial (or not so collegial) exchanges, communal ways of doing and seeing, and what gets assumed, downplayed, or bragged about.

In order to make savvy decisions about possible job offers resulting from this visit, you need to be able to imagine yourself as part of the overall scene. If the match is really good between you and the institution, this identification with the gainfully employed will seem almost effortless: Cheryl found her faculty and administrative interviewers giving her advice on writing this job search guide as if she were already a faculty mentor: "Tell them [job seekers you're advising] to. . . ." That round of interviews, by the way, ended with the question, "What will it take to bring you here?"—always a welcome question to ponder.

What to Bring to the Interview and How to Prepare and Package It

The person who calls you with the good news that you're being invited for an on-campus interview is most likely to be the department secretary. (S)he will be eager to map out the logistics of your stay: arrangements for travel and accommodations, coordinating faculty schedules with your availability, and setting up the various meetings and social activities. There are several tasks you want to accomplish at this point, some while you still have the department staffperson on the phone.

As soon as you are invited to come to campus for an interview, request that a copy of the interview itinerary be sent to you. Be sure to clarify what types of presentations you're being asked to do. If you are "teaching" a class, are class members undergraduates, a mixed audience of faculty and students, or faculty pretending to be students? Is the material to be presented one of your own lesson plans? Or should it continue the threads already woven by a particular class syllabus? Will computer or other media be available? Are handouts appropriate? Don't make the thoughtless mistake of reading a scholarly paper to a group who wants to assess your ability to engage the attention of undergraduates. You may want to request interviews with the human resources director to discuss benefits, the librarian to discuss research opportunities for you and your potential students, and the instructional technician to discuss computer access on campus.

Also clarify which travel expenses are covered. Make space on your credit cards for the expenses. Most universities will reimburse you for all of your expenses, but you pay up-front, and the check may take a while in coming. Community colleges routinely require their candidates to pay their own way. Ironically, you can't assume that campuses in financial difficulties will appreciate your footing the bill. One candidate was asked why (s)he was desperate enough to pay her own way to an institution that had apologetically told her most of its meager funds were directed at student aid! Paradoxically, a willingness to pay one's own way can send a wrong signal to your interviewers: Aren't you getting other offers? This is not true across the board (especially, as we mentioned, in the case of community colleges), but don't pay your way to an interview that severely taxes your resources or that you feel "iffy" about.

Once you get off the phone, begin preparing the materials you'll need for your visit. If you're asked to send a title for your talk and a short abstract, prepare this as if it will be distributed to the entire campus community; it probably will. This is the campus community's first encounter with the professional persona you've been constructing in conversations with the search committee. For many (especially the students) it may be their only glimpse: if your topic sounds dry or irrelevant, they may not clear space in their schedules to attend your presentation. Like the request for a corporate-style application form we urged you to take seriously in previous chapters, take the request for an abstract as another opportunity to present yourself as a valuable player.

Also prepare a teaching portfolio. This should include a list of the courses you would be interested in teaching along with corresponding working bibliographies for those courses and syllabi and writing projects for classes you have taught. Your teaching portfolio should demonstrate the range of your teaching skills. Preparing syllabi will help you articulate your sense of how you'd teach in a given institutional context, and, produced at just the right time in an interview, can show how very thoughtful and enthusiastic you are about a particular position. Don't feel compelled, however to refer to all the materials you've prepared. You may decide that, for a particular interview, the syllabi are not appropriate. You will need to decide if all of the materials you have prepared are appropriate for a particular interview.

As with the conference interview, prepare questions for those with whom you will interview on campus. Anticipate interviews with the dean, the vice president of academic affairs, and the department's faculty. Each of these will have a different focus. Be especially careful to craft clear sound bites about your specialty (service learning, computer-aided instruction, and the like) for the non-specialists you'll meet in administration. If you have the opportunity to meet with junior faculty individually, you may ask about the department's tenure record or more personal questions: What is it like to be a woman in this department, a white male, a person of color? If you can meet with students informally (say, in the library or student union building), ask them about their impressions of the institution's programs. Your research into websites and mission statements is especially important during on-campus interviews. The information you gather there about specific missions and goals can help you get a feel for how the institution views itself. If the university is undergoing changes, or stresses a particular program or goal in any of its statements, ask for different takes on its impact. For example, at a university undergoing a major structural revision, a candidate for a tenure-track position asked various echelons of interviewers questions like the following:

- How do these changes affect less secure (non tenure-track) faculty?
- How do long-term staff feel about bringing in a new Ph.D. for this position?
- How might the changes underway affect funding for specific programs or support for research?

Finally, as Associate Professor of Humanities Michael Day advises:

> Do not apply for and go on campus interviews for jobs which you are not completely sure you are interested in taking. I saw one colleague waste a lot of time and money of the interviewing schools when he went on paid interviews at those schools without first asking his wife if she would even live in those areas. As it turned out, she didn't want to live in those places, and never wanted to, and he could have saved those schools time and money by finding out from his wife and taking himself out of the running.

The Rhetoric of the On-campus Interview Schedule

You can expect your on-campus interview to include some or all of the following elements: meetings with the search committee, a tour of the campus (and sometimes the surrounding community), informal gatherings or formal meals with available faculty members and students, interviews with administrators and an extended teaching or research presentation. Some candidates in the sciences may find their campus visit structured around visits to the labs. One of our contributors in the sciences told us, "Serious negotiations over lab space go on during the interview process. Typically, what you're shown is what you get." Each of these on-campus interview components is geared to assess a different part of your fit for the job: your style of interaction with colleagues, your feel for the geographic area, your rapport with the students, your fit with the bureaucratic and administrative structure, and your ability to communicate the cache of specialized information you've become so expert in over your graduate years. This can feel like you're constantly under scrutiny; however, remember that your visit is sandwiched into schedules already full of professional, social, and personal obligations, and your audience is not as focused and unforgiving as you may imagine. Assistant Professor of Psychology Wesley Schultz notes,

> When I was the candidate, I thought everything was personal, that people were always thinking about me and evaluating me. The faculty are too busy to be that personally involved. They are looking for someone who fills the slot, that is a good fit with the program, that has the background. If they like you, that's a bonus.

In fact, by the time an institution is willing to spend the money and the effort to bring candidates to campus, it has a big stake in ultimately justifying that expense by hiring one of them. As we have mentioned before, your interview is not (or should not be) an antagonistic dialectical "defense" of your qualifications or research (although in highly politicized environments that can, unfortunately, happen), but rather a concerted attempt to discern a good match.

To help you anticipate a campus interview, here's a typical itinerary for an on-campus visit:

FIRST EVENING:

Search committee representative meets you at airport and takes you to dinner and then your hotel accommodations.

FIRST FULL DAY:

8:00 a.m.	General tour of campus
9:00 a.m.	Meet with search committee
10:00 a.m.	Presentation to faculty and students
11:00 a.m.	Meet with Director of Academic Affairs
12:00	Lunch with search committee and Faculty
2:00 p.m.	Tour of nearby community

SECOND FULL DAY:

8:00 a.m.	Breakfast with the search committee
9:00 a.m.	Meet with College Dean
10:00 a.m.	Meet with Library Acquisitions Editor

11:00 a.m.	Tour of student services programs (Writing Center, Math Lab, Aspire Program, or other student services program)
12:00	Lunch with students
1:00 p.m.	Tour of campus research facilities (lab space and computer lab)
2:00 p.m.	Meet with lab technicians and student assistants
3:00 p.m.	Meet with Human Resources Director

As contributor Kass Fleisher would tell you, such schedules leave little time for peeing (even if you are under doctor's orders to do so), much less contemplation:

> An hour before [the pedagogy presentation], I am placed in the empty office of a faculty member who happens to be on sabbatical, so that I might pull myself together and "review my notes." Notes? Hmm. The first thing I do is pee and drink a little water, which I haven't been able to do all day, since, despite gentle pleading, I am unable to get to a restroom often enough. Can't risk drinking. I remember my doctor's scolding and think, *What do you expect me to do? Make pee demands?*

Assistant Professor of English Robert D. Sturr recalls how a packed itinerary affected his on-campus interview: "I lost my voice during the day. Everything was piled into one day, so my voice was completely gone by the time we went out to dinner."

Because the university is paying for every minute you stay, the campus interview is geared towards getting you connected with the most people in the shortest amount of time. Often, committee members feel responsible for filling up unscheduled "down time." A junior faculty member, for example, may invite you to lunch, a local native will offer to show you the area, or an administrator may tell you how you can meet students in a less structured environment. Such additions to your already packed schedule are not (usually) meant as stress tests. Most often, they are sincere offers of companionship and enlightenment. Like gracious hosts, committee members want to make sure your stay is a pleasant and productive one. Robert D. Sturr reports that, during his first year as an assistant professor, he actively sought out opportunities to meet informally with candidates for an upcoming hire:

> I wasn't on the committee, but I helped in hosting candidates, and I thought that was useful. I was able to say some things to people on the side (or while driving them to interviews at the campus) that maybe others wouldn't tell them. I think it's essential for candidates to have contacts like that—new people who might be free with their comments.

While of course you want to accommodate as many helpful suggestions as possible, you also want to make sure you have time to think about the implications of what you're doing. It's perfectly appropriate to ask for time alone. Dawn, for instance, used "bathroom" breaks to study her notes in between interview sessions. When Cheryl's search-committee host rather apologetically told her she'd be alone for a morning while he attended church, he suggested she have breakfast at a very nice restaurant at the university's expense. She elected to stay in her hotel room, sipping tea and watching it rain (a treat for someone raised in arid Texas). When her host later asked her how she'd enjoyed the restaurant, he was delighted to hear she'd spent a contemplative, autonomous morning not needing to be entertained. This interchange, we might add, enriched his picture of her personality to a greater extent than would have a dutiful, "Very nice restaurant, very nice view"—just as the next year's candidate's request for a trip to the mall told them a lot about her way of exploring an area.

Consider what's being offered in invitations to activities not on the official schedule. The junior faculty member who invites you to lunch one-on-one may want to give you an insider's view of the campus. One contributor, in fact, was taken aside by a potential colleague and told, "You don't want to work here. The rest of us would leave if we could." Usually, the information junior colleagues give you isn't quite so blatant, or disconcerting. The junior faculty member may simply want to see what this new potential office mate is like "off stage." If you're able to stand one more interaction, a friendly unofficial chat over lunch can be very helpful in discerning your fit with the work environment. Interchanges there are much less official and questions about the computer lab, research labs, library, or learning center don't generally carry the same burden to give you a "binding" answer as questions asked during scheduled performances. However, always keep in mind that you're never "off the record." Don't unburden your deepest secrets even to a very open lunch companion. There will be plenty of time to form friendships if you get the job; at this point, you want to maintain a stance of friendly professionalism.

The administrator or search committee member who recommends you talk with computer lab personnel, or spend time in the library, may be responding to an interest you've expressed in part of campus operations. These contacts can add real depth to your knowledge base and can help you decide between competing job offers should that welcome situation arise. If you do meet with these people, be aware that they are setting aside their other activities to talk to you. If you don't have pressing concerns in their arena, don't try to manufacture questions to please them. A detailed training session in using the library database can come after you get the job; for now, limit yourself to a quick overview of the library's holdings, perhaps with questions like, "I often use this sort of document in my research. How would I go about getting that here?" Finally, don't overstate your enthusiasm for support staff's area of expertise. One unsuccessful candidate, for example, literally squealed when shown the school's computer lab. This unsettled the technical staff: they later questioned search committee members in hushed tones about faculty impressions of such a reaction.

The search committee member who suggests an unscheduled meeting with students might be dutifully handing you a standard line that committee members tell all applicants. A committee member who is impressed with your candidacy, however, may be hinting that you need a clearer picture of the student population. If the "talk to the students" suggestion comes before your teaching presentation, it may be that you need to make some adjustments in the way you plan to present your material. Make an effort to meet with students so you can assess your upcoming audience, and then look for ways to reach that audience more effectively. If you find in talking with students that you've read the student audience accurately, you'll go into your presentation much more confidently—and with potential allies dotting the hall. If the suggestion to meet with students one-on-one comes *after* your presentation, you might be getting a friendly hint that your scholarship was sound, but your presentation style was off-track. Again, meet with the students to be sure you have an accurate picture of what it would be like to teach at this institution.

In short, read the interview schedule as a set of rhetorical clues, and soak up any opportunity you feel will augment your ability to make decisions about a possible job offer, but don't feel obligated to do everything that is suggested. Make pee demands! If the schedule is so packed, or so convoluted and inconvenient, that it actually militates against assessing what you're seeing, or requesting additional information, beware. You want to be able to discern accurately what it would be like to become part of that campus community. If, as in several of our contributors' experiences, the itinerary has you running around barely making connecting flights or shoved into meetings directly from long drives, with no consideration for your bodily and mental health needs, interrogate your intuitive responses to this. Do you feel welcomed and wooed, or rushed like cattle through a rodeo chute?

The Rhetoric of Questions Particular to the Campus Interview

In the faculty interview, candidates can expect to be asked questions very similar to those asked at the conference. Campus interviews serve as a refresher to those search committee members who did the initial interviewing. They also allow faculty members who are not on the search committee to hear responses to key interview questions like those discussed in the previous chapter. As the candidate, you may use the "restating what you answered at the conference interview" segue to launch conversations about how your teaching, research, and community service interests will help the interviewing institution address current concerns. You want to show how your interests will help the institution problem-solve.

Your meeting with the search committee on campus at times may seem to have little purpose. If you've already discussed key items about your candidacy and the job opening during your conference interview, committee members may be hard pressed to come up with additional information to request of you. Thus, the meeting with the search committee often becomes a discussion of local concerns rather than an interrogation of your application materials, although, of course, you may be asked to talk about something you've said in your application in light of local procedures or dilemmas. The on-campus interview with the search committee is designed to take the discussion of your candidacy to a much deeper level. This interview is much more personal and specific than the conference interview. The search committee is now asking you as a potential colleague to discuss the workaday concerns of the academy. You are being consulted and, many times, wooed.

Search committee members often begin the on-campus interview by presenting information rather than asking for it. They may talk about their own personal research or teaching, about particular issues facing the campus at this time, about the organization of committees or classes, or about specific coursework that needs to be covered by the new hire. It can be a bit confusing, poised as you are to perform and to demonstrate who you are, to sit and take in this sudden flood of specific information. However, this is a good time to assess the personality of an institution. Your intuitive responses to the dialogue, presentation strategies, and chosen settings of your on-campus interviews may also give you clues as to your potential colleagues' relationships with each other, their institution, and the task of teaching/researching as a whole.

Your task during the on-campus search committee interview (and, to some extent, more casual interactions, like the campus tour and luncheon) is to assess the following issues:

- What does the committee's presentational style tell me about the way this institution operates? Is the style of communication anecdotal? Personal? A formally structured presentation of issues?

- What kinds of things do they feel I should know? Why? What don't they mention?

- What seem to be the pressing issues here? How can I address that when I make my presentation?

- Where do my interests and abilities intersect with the local issues being presented here?

- How are junior members of the faculty treated in these exchanges? Are they used as examples of mistakes that can be made, or are they encouraged to raise issues as full-fledged members of the campus community?

- How am I being constructed in this exchange? As a potential contributor? As a panting hopeful?

- What can I offer this community, and how can I communicate that as a potential colleague?

The more your style of interaction mirrors the style set up in this overture to the campus visit, the less static there will be in the way of clear communication of who you are in relation to the tasks under discussion. Here's where you begin "rehearsing" your role as colleague:

- How do you handle the very common task of sitting around a table discussing mutual concerns with other faculty members?

- How authorized do you feel to contribute?

- Are you able to listen to other's views and concerns? How do you interpret these in light of your own position?

- Do you think you have all the answers (hint: not a good strategy)?

- Can you join productively in conversations that reiterate ongoing problems, or do you feel you have to give closure and definition to everything on the table?

- How do you relate to non-faculty? An assistant professor reminds us: "In a small college, even the impressions of the secretaries and janitors may be solicited as part of the decision on who to hire. So be friendly to all; if you are hired, people will remember if you ignored them."

Rehearsals and Auditions: The On-campus Presentation

One hundred percent of the search committee members we interviewed for this book said that by far the most effective presentations are interactive. The deadliest are papers read without a glance at the audience. We realize that this moment is very important to your career, and can be terrifying to contemplate, but it's actually your place to shine. You'll be in your element, as teacher or researcher. As we noted when we first discussed looking at the entire on-campus visit as a "guest spot" in a successful production, a good match can make your "performance" memorable and intensely gratifying. Presenting an undergraduate lesson plan to faculty can seem like an epiphanic interchange with talented students. This happens when your love for the material and the discussion it generates overtakes your sense that you're performing. You've stepped completely into your "part" and have actually become the master teacher or researcher you've been training to be all those years as an "understudy."

THE TEACHING PRESENTATION

Perhaps the biggest mistake that candidates make in teaching presentations is misjudging the audience. The teaching presentation presents you with an imaginary audience: highly trained potential colleagues posing as undergraduates (sometimes mixed with real undergraduates). It's difficult not to slip into talking to these *fellow teachers and researchers* as, well, fellow teachers and researchers. Thus, it's all too easy to tell them what you'd do in the classroom instead of *demonstrating* your teaching style.

To effectively address this dual audience, situate what you're about to present before you step into your "teacherly" role. Cheryl began her presentation like this:

> I usually present this the first or second week of the semester, when students don't know each other well yet. I use it to get them talking about assumptions we make about the social context of language interactions.

Then she shifted into her character:

> You may recall that last week we talked about the language communities we all inhabit. (If you were really my students, I'd give you a quiz now, but today I'll simply go on with the lesson.) Let's talk about the metaphors we use intuitively to explain common interactions in those language communities.

She asked audience members to suggest metaphors for discussion, asked if they understood key points, and gave them feedback about their responses. This allowed her audience to contextualize the lesson in an overall pedagogical framework and still presented a clear picture of her interactive style with students.

At the end of your presentation, you can again step out of your teacherly role to tell your audience what assignments or discussions might come next. Cheryl's metaphor sequence, for example, continues with students writing an extended analogy based on thinking skills learned in the "metaphor" discussion: "My mind is like. . . ." In her on-campus presentation, she showed a transparency listing some of the analogies previous students had come up with, and that led naturally into an energetic discussion among her faculty audience members about what metaphors for classroom interaction they'd seen operating with the student population at their institution. Thus, the "performance" segment slipped easily into the question and answer period and, incidentally, gave her a good insider's view of teaching at that institution.

If you sense that this level of interaction and audience response will not be appreciated, back off. Your audience really isn't made up of undergraduates, but of very busy professionals who weren't expecting to have to do more than listen to you when they walked in the door. Gauge audience response (body language, eye contact, surreptitious paper grading) to your presentation style and adjust your presentation accordingly, just as you would in the classroom. If you sense your questions are coming across as intrusive, back off and "remind" your "class" about previous discussions they've supposedly had about the material, or introduce a new concept using your visual aids.

TIPS FOR DYNAMIC TEACHING PRESENTATIONS

- If you include technology in your presentation, always bring a back-up plan for equipment that doesn't work, servers that go down, or Power Point presentations that suddenly go off-cue. Plan as if you will have no electricity and you'll be prepared for anything. Search committee members will tell you that there is nothing more painful than watching a candidate stumble through a presentation after the server goes down.

- Use a creative lesson that's worked well with real students in the past. Not only will you be able to run through it without referring to your notes, you'll have examples from previous student work to discuss in the question and answer period.

- Present one small lesson that demonstrates a key point, and later discuss what kinds of things you expect to grow out of it—especially if you can show previous students' work that evolved from your presentation of this material in another context. Don't try to present a semester's worth of work in a short period.

- Choose a stand-alone lesson for your on-campus presentation. Don't try to present the *culmination* of a semester's work: If an assignment or a discussion takes several weeks to build up to in the classroom, don't expect to jump into it abruptly in a public forum.

- If you "teach" excerpts from your dissertation, keep your imaginary audience (undergraduates) firmly in mind: You should be adept at explaining complex material to beginners in a very short space of time if you choose this route.

THE RESEARCH PRESENTATION

Contrary to what we just told you about the teaching presentation, the research presentation is precisely the moment where an excerpt from your dissertation is most appropriate. Your audience purports to be exactly what it is—a gathering of colleagues. Use the research presentation as an opportunity to showcase your skill at making your research accessible and be sure to add tidbits of why this line of research is ideal for this school. Assistant Professor of Chemistry Jacqueline Trischman, for instance, suggested the following, campus-specific references a candidate could cite in the research presentation:

- The ready availability of proper instrumentation on-site.
- Low start-up costs for your type of research.
- Opportunities to involve undergraduates in research.
- The cutting edge aspects of your projects.
- Links to other departments.

If you've been giving conference presentations all along, you're already accustomed to encapsulating bits of your research into brief, discussion-provoking chunks that can be delivered orally. You probably have your own system of marking key words in your back-up text and for finding your place again once you've looked up to make an extraneous point. You may have even practiced performing multimedia presentations. Since your research presentation will most likely be part of your dissertation, you will also have talked about the material repeatedly, in different configurations, with different audiences and varying intents as your writing developed. So, you know your material quite well, and have already practiced delivering it in public.

However, the rhetorical task of the research presentation is not identical to the conference presentation. Whereas the conference presentation aims only at getting information across and (when things go well) generating a discussion with colleagues, the research presentation is geared to showing something about your own professional style, as well. Associate Professor of Management Regina Eisenbach tells us that, in her discipline, candidates are *expected* to present their scholarship at on-campus interviews. She encourages candidates to focus on making the paper presentation interest-ing and accessible to the widest range of potential hearers: from the under-graduate with no coursework in the major to the senior faculty member in the discipline. As Eisbenbach points out, candidates who are able to make their research presentations accessible and interesting to faculty and stu-dents alike are also demonstrating their teaching skill. In other words, your research presentation should simultaneously be a teaching moment.

One professor we interviewed offers a good example of a "teachable moment" that occurred in one of her on-campus research presentations. Just as she began to explain the significance of the data on the overhead she presented, an audience member raised her hand to point out an error in the data. The presenter admits to feeling embarrassed at first, but says that she decided rather quickly to use her typo as a teachable moment. She played into the comment by saying, "I have made this presentation three times and you are the first person to bring that error to my attention. That error has implications for my analysis. Let me show you what some of those implica-tions mean for my research results." Rather than crumbling in chagrin or slinking off in utter failure, this candidate took charge of seemingly being "caught out." She showed how she could think on her feet, and how she could teach through those awkward moments. Cheryl calls this a "good save" when she teaches interviewing to her undergraduate social science writers.

The best research presentations, then, show how teaching and research connect. And, if you can draw community service into this mix (as in, for example, a dissertation on professional issues backed up by related service in the academy, as our contributor Alan Kalish has done) you are way ahead of your competition. Since, as we discussed above, your dissertation research will probably already have generated several possible presentations for you, your task in crafting the research presentation is adding that personal/rela-tional dimension to the intellectual content already extant. How can you be personable, intellectual, and even entertaining and still communicate vital information to a large group of people in a short space of time?

Leonard Bernstein, the late conductor of the New York Philharmonic Orchestra, was a master at this. His "Young People's Concerts," which spanned the late 50's through the early 70's, lured a generation of children into thinking about tricky bits of musical "rhetoric" such as intervals, modes, and bitonality. We strongly recommend watching videotapes of these con-certs, especially the later ones: they demonstrate a clear, passionate, accessible presentation of small scholarly treasures (see appendix 5 for titles). Bernstein is clearly in love with his subject, his medium (the orchestra), and his audience, and his obvious delight in drawing the three together absolutely radiates from his tiny podium. Incredibly, camera pans of the audience show that he has the rapt cooperation of his small, squirmy auditors. What is he doing? What can *you* do without a teleprompter and the New York Philharmonic to back you up during your presentation?

HOW TO "CONDUCT" YOUR RESEARCH PRESENTATION

- Choose a manageable chunk of your very complex subject to share with your listeners. Don't try to get too much information in too small a time slot. (Bernstein often took an entire hour's program to explain one musical concept.)

- Choose material that you've used before, preferably that you've presented in different conference and classroom settings.

- Present material you will enjoy talking about. Try to find a part of your dissertation that you still accost people to talk about at parties.

- Remember that people recall only a small portion of what they hear; some researchers say information is only remembered once it's been repeated five times. If your argument is really complex, give your audience a painfully clear frame to hang it on.

- Prepare good notes, and refer to them when you need to, but don't perform a formal "reading." (Bernstein left his notes casually on the piano and, in later concerts, seemed to use them only as launching points.)

- Back up your points with visual or experiential media (your Philharmonic).

- Tie in complex ideas to ones your audience is already familiar with. (Bernstein often—seemingly on impulse—leaned over the piano and played a popular song or advertising jingle to illustrate complex terms like the "mixolydian" mode.)

- Step into your role as "conductor." Rather than presenting information in a linear path from you to your (ostensible) judges, think about inviting the audience to participate in your enthusiasm for a topic you've explored in some depth. Make your presentation a communication triangle among your material, your media, and your audience.

If you relate only to your audience, you're relying on the component of this triangle over which you have the least control.

Meeting Mr. DeMille: The Interview with the Administration

A much less public appearance is your series of talks with university administrators. Whom you talk to depends on how the system in which you're interviewing is configured. Many state universities, for example, have "satellite" campuses which interview their own candidates, then send promising prospects to the main campus for the bulk of the administrative or bureaucratic parts. If the main campus is some distance away from the campus on which you're interviewing, this will probably mean a drive (by yourself or with one of the search committee members), another night in a different hotel, and a new set of interviewers and campus maps.

A candidate interviewing at this type of structure may meet with the search committee, faculty, and students; give a teaching presentation; and talk with the director of academic affairs at the satellite campus, then drive to the main campus. The next day, (s)he may meet with the head of the department; the administrative representative of the satellite campuses; and several deans with different areas of responsibility. (S)he will probably get a tour of both campuses.

A university with all its administration centralized on one campus will most likely send you to the dean and the vice president for interviews. At a campus configured this way, a candidate may meet with faculty and students, the dean, and the vice president of academic affairs all at one campus location.

DON'T BE AFRAID OF THE SUITS

What the impressive titles signal is that these people are operating on the business end of the university. Because they aren't necessarily conversant with the latest jargon in your discipline, you may have to explain terms that have become transparent to you. (One candidate, for example, had to explain "Service Learning" to an administrator, who was then very enthusiastic about the concept and talked about how it fit in with campus projects already in play.) Some administrators will be more closely connected to actual teaching and research than others, but overall, administrators will want to look at your candidacy at the level of institutional mission, policy, and programs. Some will uphold whatever decision the hiring department or campus makes; others exert influence over that decision. This set of interviewers is not as eager to hear about a candidate's specific research interests as in hearing the candidate contextualize the research within the mission of the university as a whole.

Here are some questions our contributors have been asked in interviews with administrators:

- "How do you handle [given situation] in the classroom?"
- "What do you think of [name of text for which candidate has written a review]?"
- "I haven't had time to read your packet, but tell me about your dissertation."
- "How does your dissertation constitute research in [name of discipline]?"
- "What kinds of things are you interested in?"
- "What software/hardware do you use with your laptop?"
- "I'm interested in that project you did at State College. Tell me more about it."
- "Tell me who you are as a teacher/researcher."
- "We want to strengthen our writing curriculum; here are the snags."
- "How do your community service and research intersect?"

If these types of questions and response-gathering statements sound strangely familiar to you, you've probably been reading some of the business-oriented interview guides listed in the *Job Search* appendix. The corporate management interview *invented* questions like these. This is where the trade publications in business we've suggested will really help you. The more at home you are in a corporate setting, the more at ease you'll feel in the overtly hierarchical setup of the university administrative office. The most comfortable candidates in administrative interviews are, in fact, people who have had experience in the business world before coming to the academy.

Administrative interviewers can give you a sense of the job the university is really asking you to do. The dean who asked about laptop software and hardware, for instance, was the driving force behind a project to help faculty bring technology into the classroom. He was looking for ways he could fund this candidate's interest in computer-mediated pedagogies with the program funds he had available. The interviewer who spoke about curriculum changes also discussed possible opponents to the changes and implied the candidate would have to assert authority quite firmly in the position under discussion.

You ask administrators much the same types of questions you would other groups of interviewers. The suggestions we make below for questions to ask of the dean and vice president are not intended to be prescriptive. Your goal is not to ask each administrator all of these questions. Instead, you want to be certain that by the end of your campus interview all of your administrative questions collectively have been answered. Ask the dean at the research university questions about the college's commitment to your discipline, about other departments' professional relationships with the department you may be asked to join, about travel funds, and about the university's definitions of research and community service. At the community college, you will primarily ask questions about the institution's definition of teaching and community service. Ask the vice president of academic affairs questions about the university's perception of the department, about the relationship between faculty and administrators, or about the university's role(s) in the surrounding community. Be sure to frame questions about potentially tender areas in a non-accusatory way.

A candidate who prepares well for the other steps of the on-campus interview is prepared for the administrative interview, as well. More importantly, understand the setting (business) and the focus (the institutional mission) that underlies this group of discussions. Think back to the formal language used in the job announcement and to the legal and programmatic strictures under which the opening had to be announced (see chapter 1). You'll then have a good idea of the level of focus you should aim for in your questions and answers to their questions. The administration wants to get a sense that you understand the university's larger mission, not simply the particular job for which you're interviewing. You want to show that you value what the university as a whole values: "I understand that the university's mission is research (or teaching, or reaching a particular student population), and I can contribute in these ways."

The motive behind the questions you ask at any level should not be to impress your interviewers, to confront institutional representatives, or even to ask the "right" questions, but rather to gain information you need to make an enlightened decision about job offers that may result from your visit. Remember that at the campus interview, your audience changes frequently. You will move from a conversational breakfast meeting to a formal meeting with an administrator to a classroom presentation with only students present. As you know, you will modify your presentational style for each of these meetings.

Summary

- In the euphoria of being invited on-campus, don't forget to ask for clear instructions about practical things like travel costs and your on-campus itinerary.
- Expect to pay "up front" for travel expenses and be reimbursed later in all but community college interviews; think twice about requests to foot the bill for your own interview.
- Read the interview schedule critically. What does it say about how the institution treats its faculty?
- Consider possible reasons behind, or benefits from, suggested additions to your scheduled activities.
- Don't gush to prove your interest in the job or the facilities; let your reactions be honest and professional.
- Don't flirt with committee members, or, conversely, dismiss anyone you meet as unimportant.
- Be sure to craft your presentation for the focus and the audience you will address. Begin acting like the teacher/researcher/colleague you hope to become.
- Don't be afraid of "the suits" in administration. They're the university's corporate center.

4

REHEARSING FOR
AD-LIBBING

Preparing for (Un)Anticipated Interview Questions

Scene I

A job candidate is invited to interview on campus for what seems to be the ideal job for her particular training, specialization, and pedagogical orientation. The position announcement stressed, visually and verbally, that teaching was the primary criterion by which candidates would be judged (one of her main objectives, as well). Early telephone conversations with the dean confirmed that impression. Yet, as arrangements are made and remade for her campus visit, the candidate becomes increasingly uneasy. Despite the apparent support she senses from many sides (even to the point of being warned of potential stress tactics which might be used during her oral presentation to the department), she struggles with vague, but powerful and growing, misgivings about the situation. After many attempts to explain her seemingly unfounded angst to mentors and friends, she realizes that even an interview on campus will not clarify matters for her. She withdraws her application from consideration. The dean, confused and offended, tells her, "We probably won't hire anyone this year. You were our best candidate."

Was she experiencing pre-interview jitters? A sudden attack of arrogance? Warning signals from the deities that look after job candidates?

Scene II

In telephone and campus interviews with another institution, this same job seeker faced a different type of quandary. A position that to all outward appearances was a nightmare (one of her mentors told her, "Turn your back on this and run!") was strangely compelling to her. Despite state mandates seemingly designed to curtail student success, a student population that was woefully underprepared, and a relaxed (some would say "inefficient") style of processing candidates, the candidate found the position challenging and her would-be colleagues charming. She later reported to friends that she spent the four days on campus mentally bouncing back and forth between, "I have just entered the Twilight Zone" and "I could really make a difference here." Whether or not she could have constructed a professional self within a system whose logic and structures were bizarre is now moot; she had already begun a local one-year position by the time the call-back came, and the school insisted on an immediate start date. Yet, she would have accepted their job offer had she been able to.

Was this a narrow escape from certain misery? A tragic loss of a unique, fulfilling position? A cosmic sign not to apply to schools in that geographic area?

* * *

In a highly competitive, uncertain job market, the way you interpret each situation and the decisions made on the basis of those interpretations carry lasting material consequences. In your own job search, how might you handle situations that depend upon interpreting a complex, contradictory array of evidence? What can you do when the consensus of your mentors, friends, institution, or profession conflicts with your internal sense of the way things work? Is it naive to ignore the advice of those who are already performing in the careers you think you want, or is it courting disaster to ignore your own gut-level early warning signals?

While our own job searches and the narratives supplied by our contributors may make the search process sound simple and uneventful, our collective job search experiences have convinced us that our profession needs to address gaps between how theory gets read and how theory gets applied to our own interactions in language communities. Given the obvious need for the application of this theory, it seems ironic that many of our contributors reported that their proposals to provide interview workshops and similar "real world" applications of rhetorical theory were rejected by national conferences whose mission statements decry the abysmal state of the current job market. As contributor Patrick McCord—soon facing his first foray into the job market—told us, "I am appalled at the collective denial our profession appears to be in regarding the admissions, training, employment, and status of graduate students." Chapter 4 directly applies rhetorical theory to real-life language interactions common to the academic job search.

We believe the personal narrative is not just personal. Cultural and theoretical constructs get acted out in material space by individuals with particular histories. Have you, for instance, thought about how you might respond to questions such as the following:

- For an institution that doesn't resemble the one in which you trained:

Interviewer: "Surely someone from New York/the West Coast/a large research university would get bored teaching here."

- For an opening in composition:

Interviewer: "I just hate teaching composition, don't you? But I know the job market for teaching/doing Literature is quite dismal."

- For a biology opening at a small teaching university:

Interviewer: "Don't you believe that conducting research at a small campus like this one is really an oxymoron? Why would you want a job here?"

- For a generalist opening:

Interviewer: "How would you feel about working at an ethnically mixed/all-female/urban/teaching-oriented institution?"

Each of these questions carries within it an inherent rhetorical snag—most likely unintentional on the interviewer's part, but potentially deadly, nonetheless. Each embeds troublesome assumptions about the candidate or the job within its very sentence structure and plays havoc with the social etiquette of the interview scene. The grammar of the last question, in fact, almost requires a suicidal "I wouldn't mind" as a response. The candidate is faced with the task of communicating accurate information about her candidacy while defending intangible, largely unprovable affective states (enthusiasm, commitment to the discipline, openness to diversity), and, in an odd twist, justifying the affective states and practices of the institution to which she's applying.

The scenarios below present rhetorical snags throughout the interview process, moments when you will feel trapped. We encourage you to practice these scenarios as mock interviews. Doing so will help you prepare for unanticipated interview static. The responses we discuss are not meant to become your stock answers—scripted answers are interview suicide. Even the business question-and-answer guides listed in our appendix 5 will tell you that interviewers recognize—and despise—stock answers when they hear them. Your task is to prepare for your interviews in such a way that you can clearly articulate who you are and what you hope to do professionally. Despite what questions get thrown at you, responding fairly and respectfully will get you through the worst interview snags with your self-esteem intact.

Our suggested responses, then, give you broad genres of possible answers. You'll note that many response sequences move from the relatively innocuous to the decidedly risky. You will have to decide what level of risk you want to take at a given rhetorical turn. You don't have to be consistently risky or safe in your responses. Your own scholastic skills and passions and the kinds of experiences you've encountered will influence how you negotiate the rhetorical binds of the interview process.

SCENARIO 1

Scene: Assume you are at your disciplinary conference.

Interviewer: "So tell me about your dissertation?"

Your response: You speak for a few minutes about the dissertation. Then the interviewer interrupts you by asking a question about a professor in your department whom you have intentionally excluded from your dissertation committee due to philosophical differences. This professor does important work in your field.

Interviewer: "Who are the experts in your area on your campus?"

Candidate: Speaks about her committee members, but excludes Professor D—, the professor with whom she doesn't agree.

Interviewer: "Oh, so you have worked with Prof. D.?"

(Or)

"You didn't work with Professor D.? She's in your field, correct? Why aren't you working with him/her?"

(Or)

"You didn't mention Prof. D. You must have worked with her."

The first question in this scenario is so broad that you could answer almost anything. To complicate matters, you don't know its intention. It may be a friendly invitation to discuss your work. This is where you will be pleased that you have prepared a brief dissertation abstract, as we advised in chapters 2 and 3. The second question tightens the focus by asking for the names of specific mentors. You can simply provide a straightforward list of the appropriate faculty and what, if anything, they contributed to your work.

Responding to the final question in this scenario will require close attention to the interview environment. It has a confrontational tone; it clearly expects you to take a stand regarding your philosophical and professional alliances. The interviewer is practicing a mean-spirited version of the Socratic method, and your tasks are to assess quickly why this type of question is being asked and to determine how you want to present yourself in response. If you have excluded a potential mentor from your committee for philosophical or personal reasons, be ready to explain that non-defensively. Even if this scholar's credentials make him or her the logical choice to oversee your research, have theoretically sound reasons for this exclusion. Here are some possible responses:

- "Professor D. is certainly an outstanding scholar in this field, but I found that the work of [another outstanding scholar in the field] gave me a better frame for my particular project."

- "I took a seminar in [name of topic] with Professor D., but by the time she came on board, I had already constituted my committee/almost completed my coursework."

- "Professor D. has certainly done some interesting work in [name specific area], but I really am troubled by the ways the theory gets implemented in the classroom."

Obviously, this last response is the most direct, and it exposes you the most to potential criticism from an interviewer who considers him or herself to be a colleague of Professor D.'s. Use it only if the interviewer won't take any other answer.

SCENARIO 2

Scene: Assume you are at a conference interview for a small, teaching-oriented school.

Faculty: "Your cover letter suggests that you are proud of your research. You might not be happy here. Why do you want to work at a small place like this?"

(Or)

"Aren't you going to miss New York/the West Coast/the urban environment?"

Faculty who ask this kind of question probably are looking for a new colleague who will become a vital part of the campus community. They want you to come and stay. They probably have been burned by promising candidates from big research schools or urban centers who accepted a position, only to leave it a short time later. This sort of turn-around can be devastating to a small community of colleagues. This makes them hyper-aware of small cues that suggest you do or don't "belong" at their type of institution.

If you, in fact, want to be at this small school, you will need to translate how your research-oriented credentials or your urban background support that interest. You can't just say, "I've always wanted to teach at a small college." That will not suffice in this market, and it also doesn't seem to line up with your decision to spend five or more years at big research university in an urban area. As Assistant Professor of English Sandra H. Petrulionis told us,

> Be prepared for questions concerning what kind of students you've taught, what kind of place you like to live in, why you'd like to live there, etc. Especially if you're from New York City and you're interviewing in the middle of a small town in Texas, you need to expect to get questions regarding how well you'll be suited to and satisfied living in such a widely different place. Answer honestly, but positively.

Here are ways in which successful candidates have quite honestly handled this precarious question:

- "I spent five years in a congested, expensive, smoggy city while I was earning this degree. Now I want to get back to the type of place I really prefer: a small, close-knit community."

- "I imagine there will be things I'll miss about New York, but your location will allow me to. . . ."

- "Since you have Internet access, I'd be connected to the colleagues and materials I need to do the kind of research I do."

- "I earned my Ph.D. at a research institute, but I earned my B.A. and M.A. at a liberal arts college much like this. I particularly enjoyed. . . ."

- "I trained at a research university, but I've taught part-time at the community college throughout my time there. That student population is where my interest really lies."

If you're unsure why you applied to this type of school, this question should force you to become self-aware about why you applied here. Did you agree to this interview because it was the first (or only) call back, or are you genuinely interested in teaching at a small school? You need to be able to articulate this for yourself so that you can campaign honestly and effectively for your candidacy in these settings.

SCENARIO 3

Scene: You are on the telephone with the search committee chair making arrangements for your campus visit.

Search Chair: "You are my favorite candidate. The question we want you to address in your on-campus presentation is this: How does your experience (or, in your case, *lack* of it) make you the best candidate for this job?"

The chair's statement is obviously sending a mixed message: this candidate is an inexperienced (?) *favorite* (?) candidate. The chair may think (s)he is kindly assisting you by telling you that you are the school's first choice and by giving you insider knowledge about the campus presentation, but (s)he is also attacking your credibility. If you really do have limited experience, and the campus invites you to come, it may be that they see you as someone who can develop the requisite skills on the job. Some schools prefer less experienced candidates because they want them to design a local program that's uniquely responsive to that school. An experienced candidate may be more likely to bring in preconceived ideas based on their experience at other sites. The chair's statement, then, is not necessarily negative, but it should signal you that you need to prepare savvy ways to talk about the skills you have and how they can help you do the job. Your "lack of" experience can be presented as a stage in professional development, and your presentation can speak to the ways in which you are developing your skills.

If, in fact, you are experienced (according to the comments made by search committees on other campuses), this kind of statement should signal that your credentials are being misread. Your task in the campus presentation, then, is to translate your skills for that audience. You may decide to question the chair further about this apparent misreading. You may even decide to withdraw from the applicant pool if you think the assessment of the voting faculty can't be corrected by a campus visit. You may decide that it's simply too much work to translate your value to this group of people. This campus may just not be a good fit.

SCENARIO 4

Scene: You are at a campus interview. The interview has begun. A seemingly important person comes late (no apologies).

Late Faculty: "I haven't read your application. How does your research fit your field?"

This committee member's behavior may appear rude, but (s)he may be squeezing this in to a really packed schedule. His or her very presence may indicate that (s)he really wants to meet you. It's always better to assume this sort of scenario than take offense at a seeming disregard for your candidacy. Whether the interviewer is rude, trying to introduce stress into the interview, or (we hope) terribly busy but genuinely interested in your candidacy, you should respond to the part of the question that actually requests information. Your answer would then respond to "How does your research fit your field?" Also note that this type of question asks for a level of generality that allows you to situate yourself in the field as a whole. Again, preparation and articulation are key.

SCENARIO 5

Scene: On-campus interview with students.

Student Interviewer: "How would feel about working at our [two-year/historically black/all-women's/religiously-affiliated] college?"

As we told you earlier, the structure of this question sets you up to give a negative response. "I wouldn't mind," the expected social response, will almost certainly lose you the respect of anyone in the particular group you cite. We encourage you instead to use this interview opportunity to state positively why you chose to apply to this school:

- "My part-time teaching at a similar school convinced me that I wanted to continue working with this student population once I earned my Ph.D."

- "Excited, elated, challenged, fulfilled, intellectually stimulated. . . ." (Be sure you know how to explain *why* you'd feel this way).

To avoid the inherent rhetorical snags in questions of this type, you need implicitly to rewrite the question in your response. You want to show you're excited about the possibilities at this campus, but you don't want to appear as the great philanthropist, slumming until (s)he receives a position at a school with a broader-based student population.

SCENARIO 6

Scene: The Dean's office. Your *vita* indicates that you do ethnic studies research and teaching.

Interviewer: "Your *vita* suggests that you are interested in ethnic studies. What does that mean?"

Candidate: Speaks for several minutes.

Interviewer: (interrupting) "No, what brought *you* to ethnic studies?

Again, the first question may be a friendly invitation to discuss your scholarship and pedagogy. It also may be a valid request for information—especially if you're being interviewed by administrators who want a general understanding of you in relation to your field. Given the sensitive nature of these areas of specialization, questions about your commitment to these areas can be unwittingly invasive. Don't feel like you have to respond with details about your family history, your ethnicity, gender, or sexual orientation.

- "I'm drawn to the way women's experiences get packaged and I love the writers' freedom to talk about things that were once considered unimportant or even unmentionable."

- "The theory in this field allows us understand social and relational structures in a fresh way."

- "I've come to the scholarly field as an activist. I want to find ways to remove existing economic and social barriers."

A follow-up question to this exchange might be:

Interviewer: "Our university has an [Ethnic, Multicultural, or Gender] Studies program. What would you offer to that program?"

As we told you in chapters 2 and 3, questions like these make it clear that the preparation time you invested in reviewing web pages and college catalogs, preparing relevant questions, and writing sample syllabi was time well spent.

SCENARIO 7

Scene: Telephone follow-up to official job offer. You're juggling several offers with different timetables for response.

Person extending offer: "Have you made a decision about our offer?"

You've made it through the job search, hoping for an offer, and now you have three. Your very success will likely produce awkward rhetorical moments because the offers will most likely not be on the same deadline schedules. Your task will be to field queries about your decision-making process. It may be the case that you have one contract in hand, with a decision due in a week; another contract that's in the mail; and one school—your first choice—tantalizing you with frequent calls asking if you're still interested in their opening. Of course, you want to give your first choice institution time to offer you the job and get you a contract.

> "Thank you for being so interested in my candidacy. I'm still waiting for information about the other offers I told you about. Let me contact the other search committees again and I'll try to get back to you within the next two days."

After you hang up from this call, contact your first-choice institution:

> "Thanks for your calls the last two weeks. I have received two offers from other schools, but I'm still very interested in your position. I'm wondering if the committee has had the opportunity to make their decision yet."

SCENARIO 8

Scene: Candidate-initiated telephone call to decline a job offer.

Rejecting a job offer can be awkward because you want to be appreciative, respectful, definite, and yet you want to leave the lines of communication open. While you don't have to explain specifics about why you're not accepting an offer, if you have established a good relationship with search committee members, you may want to have a short, collegial conversation.

- "Thank you very much for your offer. I've decided to accept another position."

- "This was a difficult decision for me to make, but I've decided to accept another position. I really enjoyed getting to know the faculty on your campus during the interview process. Thank you for your offer."

- "Thank you very much for your offer, but I've decided that a postdoc is the best option for me at this point in my career. I'd really like to keep in touch with you, because I think we share a lot of interests."

Tricky Cues for Ad-Libs

Several contributors reported real-life tricky rhetorical situations from their own interview experiences. We share them here to help you imagine additional practice scenarios which can help you rehearse for your own ad-libs.

STRESS TACTICS

An assistant professor at a community college adds his experience with stress tactics during an on-campus interview:

> Having spent thirty minutes writing an essay about a well-known author, ten minutes marking a sample student essay, and forty-five minutes in the interview, I was handed a sheet of paper which simply read: You have ten minutes to prepare a fifteen-minute teaching demonstration on one of the following topics—the period, the comma, or transitions.

Assistant Professor of Psychology Wesley Schultz recalls what made interview questions tough:

> The questions aren't tough because they are scholarly or somehow asking about theoretical assumptions. They are tough because there is an agenda. For instance, when I interviewed at one university they had an environmental psychologist ask a question with which I completely disagreed. I knew that the question implied a whole theoretical perspective with which I disagreed. Do you want to say, "Well that is just wrong?" Do you bow and say, "That's your (the interviewer's) perspective?" Or do you maintain your own position? Is he testing me to see if I know that perspective? Or is he testing me to see where my allegiances are?

Schultz realized there were rhetorical maneuvers implied by this genre of question, but he decided to base his answers on his understanding of the research in the field rather than attempt to dance around more politically grounded implications. In another interview, Schultz recalls:

> I interviewed at State U. State U does the touchy feely stuff. They were looking for a statistician. I presented heavy duty data-based statistical analysis, the latest cutting edge stuff. They sat there with their arms

crossed At the end they asked conceptual questions. Was I willing to
leave the data? I knew I was being set up.

Interviewers were trying to discern whether he was so hooked to data that
he had no other tools to respond. Could he apply the data in a more personal format?

Assistant Professor of Economics Ranjeeta Ghiara adds her discipline's
version of this dilemma:

> Most of economics is very conservative. My program was heterodox.
> There is a group of faculty who are radical political economists. In fact
> the leading journal in radical political economy is published by my
> department. I could see interviewers thinking, "Hmm, you might be a
> trouble maker."

A different sort of snag occurs when interviewer comments don't meet
the candidate's expectations. Ghiara's first interview started with a shock
because the "right" question wasn't asked:

> They told us [advisors] that interviews always began with questions
> about the dissertation. Suddenly someone asks a question about my
> teaching. Something like, "If you had a course of this kind, how would
> you design it?" It was a question that took some thought and knowl-
> edge about the school. It was like, "Hi . . . so tell us about this class."

UNEXPECTED AND FORBIDDEN QUESTIONS

- Another surprise came when interview questions didn't bear out
  Ghiara's mentor's advice: "They told us teaching schools would ask
  more teaching questions," Ghiara told us. "But for me it happened
  just the opposite."

- Assistant Professor of English Robert D. Sturr recalls his experience
  "tripping over 'forbidden' questions" during a tour of the
  community:

> They'd ask about churches I might want to see or about my "partner."
> I gather they weren't supposed to do that, but how else can you decide
> about a job? It felt absolutely necessary if my wife and I were to make
> an informed decision. I took the attitude that I was going to reveal per-

sonal information (but, of course, that's far less risky when you're a straight white male).

- Ellen M. Gil-Gomez, Assistant Professor of English, recalls her experiences with less informative illegal questions:

After interviews I was stunned by obviously "illegal" questions clearly meant to uncover my sexual behavior and/or racial identity such as: questions about my birth control practices, about my family planning, about whether I cared about the Mexican people or just books, about whether I ever benefited from affirmative action, and—my favorite— could I cook good Mexican food.

- Another candidate reports similar experiences:

There were some truly bizarre situations along the way, from listening to faculty members discuss their sex lives at interview dinners to being grilled about my parents' work history. I have a Hispanic background, and one faculty interviewer wanted to know if I had been a migrant farm worker. She was openly disappointed and put off that I hadn't. Such nitty-gritty situations aren't covered even in the best how-to guides.

- Other interviewers want to know how *you* will respond to the ethnic mix represented in their particular student population. Assistant Professor of Psychology Gina Grimshaw was asked a fairly common question in this genre, "How do you handle diversity in the classroom?"

THE "SO YOU DIDN'T GET TENURE" QUESTION

Candidates who are out on the market again after not receiving tenure face what is perhaps the most dreaded genre of questions: "Why didn't you receive tenure?" The implication—no matter how gently the question is asked—is that the candidate did something less-than-stellar to self-induce this woe. One savvy contributor, Assistant Professor of Biology Dianna L. Bourke, solved this dilemma with an equally tough answer: "I invested so much time in my teaching that I neglected to publish enough research. I didn't get tenure." If pressed for details, she outlined ways in which she had revamped a program in trouble at the expense of her own research, and mused about ways she could use this experience to balance more equitably teaching, research, and service in a similar situation. While these responses made admitting she didn't receive tenure no less painful, they gave her an opportunity to present herself as an independent thinker who was able to restrategize her own practices. She received a job at a teaching-oriented school while she was finishing up her last year at the institution that denied her tenure.

* * *

As you've probably realized by this point, you can never prepare for every sort of question that may get thrown at you. Sometimes, illegal or esteem-threatening questions are simply the result of interviewers who have received inadequate (or no) training in proper interview procedures. Other times, tricky questions give you real insight into the atmosphere you'd face if you accepted an offer from a particular institution. Our advice to you, as we've told you throughout *Job Search*, is to come prepared to articulate clearly who you are and what you want to do. If you know parts of your work experience, training, or even personal history are likely to generate inquisitive but stress-ful invasions of delicate territory, be sure to practice discussing these areas in a straightforward, professional way before you get there. The more you've practiced talking about your professional self with colleagues, the more com-fortable you will be when interviewers (however unprofessionally) ask you to do so. And, as Dawn reminded herself during her own job search, "I'm not going to be desperate in a desperate market."

Anticipated Faculty Interview Questions

Assistant Professor of English Jennifer C. Vaught generously offered the fol-lowing lists of questions she was asked and those she asked during the inter-view process. We have made minor revisions to some of these questions so that you can see even more clearly the ways you might modify the questions to fit your own disciplines:

QUESTIONS ASKED OF CANDIDATES DURING INTERVIEWS

Jennifer C. Vaught, Assistant Professor of English

1. Describe what you would include in a four-credit required course on

[Shakespeare, biophysics, algebraic theories, organizational management] for majors at the senior level?

2. How would you handle the same course if it were taught as an interactive television course? Have you any knowledge of or experience in teaching such a course?

3. Apart from your specific area of specialization, in what areas would you feel strong teaching?

4. What ideas do you have for a graduate course in your area of specialization?

5. Tell us a little about your ideas for teaching writing in your core classes.

6. Would you like to add anything about your philosophy of teaching in general?

7. Indicate how you see your dissertation and other research relating to your teaching. What are your plans for professional development? i.e. where do you see yourself in your research five years from now?

8. We teach a broad based course called "Great Books, Success and Values in the U.S."; the books are expected to stimulate thinking and discussion of humanistic values. The only requirement is that at least one book be published before 1900. What books would you select for such a course?

9. Do you have any questions about the school, the department, the position, the working conditions, the town, etc?

QUESTIONS THE CANDIDATES ASKED DURING INTERVIEWS

Jennifer C. Vaught, Assistant Professor of English

1. What are the students at this institution like?

2. What do you hope the person who is hired will do? (i.e. kinds of courses the person would teach, interest in working with the theater department, etc.)

3. What's the role of the university and your department in the community? What is the service component of the position like?

4. Is there a sense of community within the department? Do faculty

socialize together? How many adjuncts and graduate students are in the program?

5. Where are most of the students from?

6. Are there any research groups among the faculty? Do these groups include graduate students?

7. What is the relation of the university to other schools in the region?

8. What are the requirements for tenure? When do faculty members go up for tenure?

9. Is there support for research? Grants? Library resources, etc.?

10. Are there faculty colloquia within the department or other opportunities for presenting research? Are there opportunities for doing research jointly with students?

11. What are the current teaching needs in the department?

12. Do faculty members sometimes lead students on study-abroad programs through the university?

13. (Of an administrator, to get a sense of available funding): What is the relationship between the university and the state legislature?

How Business Guides Help You Anticipate Tricky Questions

Although the following list of tricky questions echoes frequently asked questions listed in almost any business job guide, you won't find these particular questions in the business guides listed in our appendix 5. We have applied our own rhetorical training and market experience to rewrite the questions most often cited in business job guides within an academic context. We encourage you to do the same with questions that apply directly to your job search. Here are twenty-five "tweaked" questions to get you started.

1. Tell us about yourself.

2. I haven't read your application packet, but tell me about your dissertation/your research/your experience/your qualifications.

3. Who/what has influenced your research/teaching development?

4. Where do you plan to be in your teaching and research in five years?

5. Why are you interested in this university?

6. Why do you want to leave your current position?

7. How have your training and experience, inside and outside the university, prepared you for this position?

8. How would you feel about working at an ethnically mixed/all-female/urban/teaching-oriented institution?

9. Tell us about a project you initiated.

10. We've all learned to critique other people's ideas. What is the most useful criticism you have received, and how did it help you?

11. How do you deal with pressure situations in the classroom?

12. Tell us about a difficult teaching decision you've made.

13. Can you give us an example of how you solve problems?

14. Describe a situation in which you had a conflict with a student, peer, or mentor.

15. Give an example of a situation in which a lesson plan failed, and how you handled it.

16. What frustrates you the most about teaching?

17. Describe two or three research accomplishments that have given you great satisfaction.

18. Tell us which characteristics are important in a good teacher and how you've displayed one of those characteristics.

19. How would you describe your teaching style?

20. How do you do your lesson/research planning?

21. How do you motivate students?

22. What kind of administrative experience have you had?

23. How are you conducting your job search, and how will you make your decision?

24. What can you contribute to our university, the field, our community?

25. We've received some 500 applications for this position. Why are you the best person for the job?

5

THE AWARDS CEREMONY
Negotiating the Job Contract

If nothing else, know that you can and should negotiate your job offer.
—Regina Eisenbach, Associate Professor of Management

The Job Offer as a Rhetorical Scene

Negotiating your job contract is the final stage of the application-to-interview job search process. It also the stage for which you are least prepared. Most of the candidates we interviewed told us things like,

- "If I had only known, I would have negotiated my contract."
- "Once I arrived on campus, it was quickly apparent to me that my most powerful moment in the institution was the time I sat with my unsigned contract in-hand."
- "The contract is not only about in-coming salary. It is about moving expenses and teaching and research tools that can help you become the teacher and researcher you intend to be."

Once you receive the offer, which usually comes from the college dean, realize that the school is telling you, "We want you to join us. Our hope is that you will come and stay." The school has invested valuable time and money in you. The search committee in particular and university community as a whole want you to feel welcomed. Part of this welcoming is providing you the most competitive offer possible. It then becomes your responsibility to remind them of why they selected you for the position.

That is what you accomplish in this final stage. The credentials you narrated during the conference or phone interview and brought to life during your campus visit are your explicit support for the requests you make during this negotiating stage. More importantly, as you review the contract, you become more aware of the kind of partnership the school imagines with you:

- Is the offer for a *tenure-track position?* (If so, you likely have considerable negotiating room.)

- Is this a *competitive tenure-track* offer? In other words, is more than one candidate being hired for the same position? If so, it is likely that within three years, the school will dismiss all but one of you. In other words, you will compete with a colleague for three years to see who keeps the position. (A competitive offer does not usually allow for much negotiating room. In this situation, the negotiating power comes after the other competitive colleagues have been dismissed.)

- Is this a *non-tenure track* offer? (If so, you may have some negotiating room, but you will have little job security.)

- Is the university or college offering a one, two, or three year *renewable contract?* (If so, you likely have little negotiating room.)

- Is this a *community college* tenure-track position? If so, you likely have little room to negotiate. The community college tends to handle contracts as a clerical project with all pieces predetermined by state and institutional regulations (hence, little negotiating space). As one community college professor told us,

There is no negotiating at the community college; not with the hiring committee or dean or anything like that. The negotiations go on with the personnel person who reviews your work and academic history and decides what credit to give you for courses taken and time served. Teaching experience determines your place in the pay scale. Units taken determine your column placement. These are negotiable only insofar as you are able to convince the person reviewing your file of your experience that is not listed on your *vita* or transcripts. That is why I worked for a month without knowing what I was making. (Remember: I was offered the job on a Friday night to begin a spring semester on Monday morning.)

The non-competitive, tenure-track offer allows for the greatest degree of negotiating. While the idea of negotiating may be displeasing to you, know that this does not need to be a dialectical (antagonistic) experience. Remember, in this conversation you are simply reminding the dean (or the person extending the offer) how you will add to their intellectual community and you are explaining what that contribution is worth.

How to Assess Institutional Environments

QUESTIONING YOURSELF AND THE JOB OFFER

The academic interview can be an exhilarating confirmation of your most deeply cherished theories, or a plunge into an existentialist void (often, simultaneously). In many of the interview experiences we've researched, candidates felt torn between what they'd been taught to want in a position and what their intuitive reactions to their interview experiences were telling them. A big discrepancy between these external and internal criteria can cloud the decision-making process with confusion and frustration. Recall the faculty interaction. As you were interviewing on campus, you were asking yourself questions like those Assistant Professor of English Sandra H. Petrulionis suggests:

> You cannot overtrust your instincts. Watch the faculty interact with each other: do they seem to get along? do they act as though they truly like one another? do they talk about subjects that let you know that they get together socially, that they know each other's families, kids, etc.? If you detect tension in the air, it's probably there. When you go to lunch or dinner, watch them talk (or not) with one another. What do they talk about? Trust your hunches. You do not want or need to work in a place where backbiting is taking place at the level of a candidate interview when everyone should be on their best behavior. If an interviewer talks to you about a colleague, watch out! It could be one bad apple, or it could be a whole orchard that's rotten.

Now that you're considering a contract, your intellectual and intuitive responses to these rhetorical scenes are crucial. As you make decisions about job offers, also return to the debriefing notes you collected after each stage of the interview process. Recall specific scenarios you experienced. As best you can, you want to remind yourself of the school's strengths and weaknesses. With those thoughts fresh in your mind (better yet, with those thoughts jotted down), ask yourself if the offer really seems to be a good fit. As you assess the fit, step out of the interview scene and ask critical questions of it.

JOB SEARCH JITTERS OR REAL WARNING BELLS?

The following guidelines, drawn from our own interview experiences and those of the people who have shared their experiences with us may help you critically read the rhetorical scene of your interview experience, an analysis that will help you make the best decision regarding the offer. They are in no particular order, and we hope that your interview experience does not require that you consider all of them when you make your decisions about the job contract. Our hope is that the questions and responses that follow help you sort out everyday "jitters" from real "warning bells."

1. *Did I feel demeaned by committee comments or interview arrangements?* Search committee comments can be, well, searching, but they should not leave a candidate feeling diminished in any way. Comments such as, "The purpose of this meeting is to give candidates the opportunity to tell us how their experience and training— or, in your case, the lack of it—equip you to teach at our university" do not serve any purpose but to intimidate. (Even if you feel desperate enough to put up with such interview tactics, do you really want such a group eventually voting on your tenure?)

   Likewise, the physical arrangements of the on-campus interview should allow you to assess the institution and its context, as well as to be assessed as a candidate. The on-campus interview from which one of the authors withdrew imagined her scrambling from red-eye flights, to long drives in rental cars, to a series of interviews, leaving no time to initiate conversations, no time to explore the surrounding city, and (ultimately) no opportunity to eat or think. Being scheduled out of these information-gathering activities betrays a certain lack of professional courtesy in an institution's administration, even if the search committee seems enthusiastic about your candidacy.

2. *Is my training or experience being misread, effaced, or ignored?* While institutions give varying weight to different types of training and work experience, and to that of different candidates, there should be some recognition of how your activities as a student stack up against those of other students. The graduate experience is anything but routine. You may have received a scholarship that freed you to concentrate solely on your own work; you may have done research with a prolific professor on his or her project; you may have handled rare manuscripts or special collections; you may have been a lead or support graduate research student in your advisor's lab; or you may have taught your own classes. Note, then, how these activities are "read." Is your role in the research you conducted clear to the interviewers? Is part-time teaching considered experience? Is your experience as a teaching assistant interpreted as "marking time"? How are publications and conference presentations talked about? If you find yourself justifying praiseworthy graduate experience, watch out. Also pay attention to the ways in which your *vita* and other dossier materials get distributed. Remember the institution that copied and distributed only page one of a five-page *vita*, then repeatedly asked the candidate why her experience was limited to the information which was listed on that page alone?

3. *Is the job description clear, or are there different readings from different committee members?* As we saw in the examples above, a faculty who can't define what position it wants filled or what the successful fulfillment of that position's requirements would look like, offers a shaky ground for eventual tenure. If the expectations of the new hire are always under revision and no single job description stands as the evaluative standard, both the interview and the tenure processes could be harrowing experiences. A committee's (in)ability to reach consensus can give you a clue to the overall atmosphere of the institution you hope to join. Since these same people will be voting on your tenure eventually, it's best that they at least agree (however grudgingly) on what your job should be.

4. *Does the faculty seem able to work together? Do I sense one faction pushing my candidacy against another, dissenting faction? What tends to settle disagreements (student interests, administrative action, group decisions)?*

While it's possible (even probable) that some faculty members will like you more than others, strong opposition—or the advocacy of one powerful figure, like a dean or chair—can make trouble at tenure time. Remember the campus interview is your opportunity to earn votes from the faculty and administrators. You, however, don't want to be the pet of the current dean and inherit his/her enemies. In addition, that powerful advocate may no longer be in a position to help you later. Similarly, some candidates cut themselves short by identifying too closely with one sympathetic committee member.

5. *Do the salary range and rank seem reasonable for an entry-level job in this particular area of the country?* National salary averages can be misleading; here, regional conditions are much more accurate. Along with the local cost of living, it's smart to find out the salary ranges for similar positions at other area colleges. That will give you a better idea of how the salary you're being offered rates in the local economy. A telephone search in one city revealed that salaries for similar positions varied as much as $6,000 a year, depending on whether the college targeted an historically underprivileged student population, whether it was funded by state or private means, or whether it lacked status in the area. Dawn learned to listen carefully to the salary range the administrators described. In conversations over coffee with potential colleagues, in her discussions with professors at nearby universities, and in her conversations with the human resource management director, she learned the salary range for a particular job was between $28,000 and $34,000. When the Dean discussed salary with her, he mentioned that the salary would be "around $32,000." Knowing the range, she knew she had some room to negotiate.

   Also consider physical or economic factors that can affect your overall perception of the rank and salary. Do poor conditions in public schools mean you'll be paying private school tuition for your children, or will high rents or energy bills cut into that projected paycheck? Conversely, does a hefty salary make an otherwise unattractive position only seem like a good job?

6. *What does my intuition tell me?* While this is the least tangible criterion, it is in many ways the most important. You can feel worried, trapped, and denigrated in an interview, with no articulable empirical cause. Or,

you can see all sorts of things in a prospective position that would make your mentors blanch, yet feel excited, challenged, creative, and energized. Here is where what your mentors would say vs. your individual perceptions of a job really duke it out. We along with the job candidates we've interviewed for this book have found that advice—however good-intentioned and firmly believed—is always rooted in someone else's experience. Helpful suggestions (including the ones in this book) spring from individual ways of seeing, and may not prove out in your experience. As you know, advice has to be read as part of a network of ways of seeing and knowing, rather than applied as authoritative in any given situation. Our hope is that the collected experiences we present help you to anticipate fully the rhetorical reality of the job search.

Receiving the Job Offer

The typical formal job offer season for universities is during March and April. However, it is likely that you have heard stories about candidates for university positions receiving late job offers. One contributor, in fact, was hired at the beginning of July for a job that started in August. Most universities finalize their budgets for the following academic year during Spring semester, so you can expect to hear from them any time from March on. Securing contracts with in-coming faculty is certainly a significant part of the budgetary planning that administrators need to complete. If your application-to-interview process follows professional etiquette, the job offer will not come as an absolute surprise, and you will have two weeks to respond to the offer. Yet, you may feel pressured into believing that you have only days to make a decision. (Note that the community college process is very much less bound by the calendar: offers can come quite literally just before teaching begins. Community college budgets are reworked right up to the end of the fiscal year in June, and many times positions only get funding approved at that late date.)

Generally, offers are extended to you in one of two rhetorical scenes:

• At the campus interview.

• By phone.

Some candidates are told at their interviews that they are the university's or college's hopeful hire. For most candidates, an offer extended during the campus interview is the most difficult one to negotiate. You may feel pressured to respond immediately or before you leave the campus visit. Know that you do not need to make your decision at this time. In fact, we encourage you to delay your decision. Remember that you usually have two weeks to respond to an offer. You want to use that time to meet with your mentor or dissertation committee to discuss the offer in full. (If your faculty haven't been good mentors, ask the advice of former classmates who have already been working in the profession for a year or so or seasoned faculty you've worked with as journal editors, collaborators, or conference organizers. This peer mentoring is especially important when your faculty mentors disagree with your choice to pursue a position at a particular institution or during a particular search cycle.)

Taking the time to consult with mentors helps you make a more savvy decision. The faculty on your committee may have information that you were not able to gather at the interview that will inform your final decision in significant ways. For instance, the faculty from your home program may know colleagues who work at the campus with whom you didn't meet who can provide the "inside scoop" about a particular campus. Your faculty "support team" may be able to direct you to former faculty of a particular campus that left the campus for particular reasons. You will want to know that information. Finally, you may be a strong candidate at other campuses which means you will have other offers to review, so you don't want to rush any one decision. Allow yourself to step back from the interview process so that you can make the best professional decision for you.

If you receive your offer the more common way, by phone, you may know that the offer is coming before the phone rings. Often, before a formal offer is made, the search committee calls your references. It is not uncommon for your references to then call you to let you know that a particular college has just called to inquire about your skill as a teacher and researcher. You may also choose to check in with your references periodically to see if universities and colleges have called them. It is very unlikely that you will simply receive a contract in the mail without prior notice.

If you receive the offer over the phone, it is typical for the person extending the offer to read the formal offer to you on the phone. Jot down significant features of the offer during this conversation, and certainly feel free to ask questions about the offer. (See "Understanding the Job Offer" below for help with what to ask). You should not, however, feel compelled to accept the offer over the phone. Instead, ask that the formal offer be faxed or mailed. Explain that you will be meeting with your chair or dissertation committee to review the offer. (If you worked in an adjunct position while you finished your dissertation, you may want to ask present-day colleagues rather than mentors who haven't seen you for awhile). You will feel wonderful about having the offer, and your enthusiasm will likely show when the university or college extends the offer. Keep reminding yourself, however, that you want to make the best decision, not a rushed decision based on your knowledge that the academic market has been especially competitive. Just because the market has been challenging doesn't mean that you don't have time to think. If you feel especially pressured to make a decision over the phone, make note of that. Unnecessary pressure at the contract stage may tell you a bit more about the institutional environment.

The Rhetoric of Negotiating a Job Offer

UNDERSTANDING THE JOB OFFER

After years of surviving on student loans and grants that have kept you just above the poverty line, you will likely want to accept the initial job offer quickly and graciously. Resist the temptation. Remember that an unsigned job offer provides you with an important kind of power—not one to be abused, but one to be used wisely.

First, determine what kind of offer is being made: tenure track, competitive tenure-track, non-tenure track renewable.

- The tenure-track contract provides you with the most room to negotiate.

- After consultation with your dissertation committee, you may decide that your *vita* and your research skills position you well to withstand the sorting process associated with an offer of the competitive tenure-track position.

- You may decide to eliminate non-tenure track offers, or consider taking a visiting position to strengthen your candidacy for a tenure-track position, as Jeanne-Marie Zeck did (see chapter 6 for a more detailed discussion of this option). Or maybe the search committee has told you that a tenure-track position will open in the next year and that internal candidates will be encouraged to apply.

• You may decide that the non-tenure-track, renewable contract offer in a particular region of the country will allow you to pursue non-academic professional opportunities.

Once you decide whether the kind of offer extended is one that you will seriously consider, read the fine print. With contract in hand, ask yourself these questions:

1. *Is the salary fair?* As we mentioned earlier in this chapter, there are several ways to research the salary range. If the college or university is public, all salaries are public which means you should have access to them. The Human Resources Management department will be able to provide you with that information. Many times the campus libraries also have that information. (During your interview, you may request to spend some time exploring in the library on your own. This would provide you with some of the privacy needed to do this research.)

2. *Do the faculty have union representation?* The union can help you determine not only a fair salary but a fair contract. You may also choose to contact the Human Resource Management departments at other campuses in the region to determine salary ranges there for incoming assistant professors in your discipline. Combining this information will help you feel more confident about your response to the offer.

3. *What is the teaching load?* Your contract should indicate your teaching load. At exclusive research universities, you might expect a 2-2 load which means you would be teaching two courses each semester. (Naturally, this light teaching load would be countered by a heavy research requirement.) If the campus is on quarters, the offer might be for a 2-2-3 load. At state universities and small liberal arts colleges, a 3-3 or 4-4 load is more typical. Finally, at community colleges, a 5-5 load is very common. (The community college is the mirror image of the research university; the heavy teaching load replaces a hefty emphasis on research.)

   Your work load should be explicit in the contract, but it can be negotiated further. You can counter a heavy teaching load in temporary ways. If, for example, faculty on the campus have a 4-4 load, it is unlikely that as an assistant professor that you will be able to ask for a 2-2 load permanently. If you, however, have just received a significant grant or book contract, you may want to ask for a 2-2 for the first year so that you can complete the research projects to which you have recently agreed. Your research will bring respect to the college or university, so the campus will likely want to work with you on this. (It is unlikely that the reverse is possible: as many tenure-track professors have found to their hurt, prioritizing teaching over research can be lethal, even if you're fulfilling a crying need at the institution).

4. *Are start-up research funds available?* Campuses want you to be able to get a running start on your research once you arrive. To help you with this, many schools will extend start-up research funds to you for you to spend in ways that will enhance your teaching or research agenda. (Most community colleges provide opportunities for district-sponsored workshops that enhance teaching). Faculty usually use these funds for special computer programs, lap tops, or other technical tools; books; research assistants; outside research expenses and the like. A respectable start-up fund for a humanities faculty candidate is $1200. However, some faculty who need to create special research labs may begin with several thousand dollars.

   One of our science colleagues confesses, "The start-up funds question was the one question I was least prepared to answer in my initial interviews. You need to know how much it would cost to set-up a productive research lab in your field." She advises, "Don't low-ball. Come prepared with two lists—the need list and the want list. Ask around to find out how much the last person hired got and try to stay in that order of magnitude. The range is typically from $10K to $300K." Again, your new colleagues or the union can help you determine what is fair for the campus at which you are negotiating.

5. *Are travel/research funds available annually?* During the university campus interview, you likely spoke with the dean about annual research funds. Are the funds made explicit in the contract? Sometimes they are. Often, they are not. The dean, however, should be able to tell you what you can expect. Know that, especially with public schools, research funds may fluctuate over the years between nothing and a few thousand dollars. Not all campuses will provide

funds. Community colleges in particular direct their faculty development funds to pedagogy rather than research. If your scholarship
depends on research money and the school cannot provide it, this
may be a clear sign that the campus is not a research campus. How
do you feel about that?

6. *What are the office arrangements?* You want to know whether you will
have your own office or if you will be sharing it with another colleague. You will want to know what kind of furniture will be available. Do you need to bring additional bookshelves or chairs? You'll
want to know this as you pack your belongings to move (While the
contract usually won't detail exactly what will be in your office, often
it mentions that you will have an office). The contract stage is a good
time then to get answers to your questions about space arrangements. You will also want to recall office arrangements that you
noted when you visited the campus. Since office space probably
won't make the difference between whether or not you accept the
offer, your queries on these items can be very low-key.

7. *Will you have an adequate computer in your office?* Most campuses rely
on computers, so you should expect a computer in your office. Often
at the contract stage, you will be asked what kind of computer you
want: a Mac or PC. You may ask to speak with the computing special-
ists on campus to determine the kind of software that is standard on
campus. If you will need additional pieces of technology like scan-
ners or Zip drives, you will want to ask. At this point, you may want
to ask whether the campus has a computer lab for faculty that provides the cutting-edge tools that you might need.

8. *What about lab space?* Is it adequate for your research? During the
campus interview, if your discipline requires research facilities, you
should have visited research labs. Do you know what kind of lab space
an assistant professor can expect? You want to know how much space
you will have, what kind of equipment you will have, and whether you
will have research assistants. Ask the faculty and the dean.

9. *Will the college or your department cover journal subscription expenses?*
Journal subscriptions are likely integral to your research. While contracts will not usually be so specific as to mention whether journal
subscription expenses are covered, the contract stage is certainly an

appropriate time to ask. It is likely that such expenses will not be covered, but possibly you can request that the campus library purchase an institutional subscription.

10. *What are the employee benefits?* While the contract will not usually detail your benefits package, it should highlight benefits such as medical and dental. To understand in full the employee benefits, you will want to talk to the Human Resources Management director. This person can provide you with details about medical and dental benefits as well as information about life, disability, and voluntary insurance; retirement plans; tax shelters; paid and family leave. Employee benefits are available at universities, colleges, and community colleges.

11. *Are relocation expenses paid?* It is not common for schools to pay for relocation expenses. More often, you will find that search committees will offer to help you move in once you arrive. You will also find that faculty are very obliging to help you find new homes, so don't be shy about letting search committees know that you will be looking for a home or apartment when you arrive to begin your new position. Some schools do offer moving expenses, though, so certainly ask. Those who can offer these kinds of funds can usually only defray expenses. In other words, don't expect that schools will cover the full expense of moving you and your family across the country. It is more realistic to expect that the school will pay from $500 to $3000 towards your moving. Be certain to keep all receipts connected to your moving, including receipts for packing materials, food, and gas. These expenses will be tax deductible.

12. *Are you expected to have your degree in hand when you arrive?* If not, is the completion date realistic? During the interview, most search committees will ask when you will have your Ph.D. in hand. Be realistic and confident here. In today's market, you shouldn't be on the market unless you expect to have the dissertation completed before you arrive on your new campus. However, remember that there is likely lag between the time that you defend your dissertation and the time that you file it. Build in time to sign the requisite paperwork and to print the final copy. It is not uncommon for schools to give you the Fall semester to finalize your dissertation and the paperwork.

* * *

Of course, some of the issues we've just discussed will not be priorities for you. You don't need to ask all of these questions of the person extending the offer. The arrival of the contract in your mailbox, however, should trigger you to read the contract critically and to sort through the questions to which *you* need real answers. In an imperfect world, what combination of conditions will make you feel like this would be a good match? You want to be aware of the features that construct the business end of your profession, but you do not want to become so hyper-aware of your "rights" that you lose touch with realistic expectations of the faculty position. We want you to get a contract that is fair to you and that works within the school's fiscal structures.

COUNTERING THE JOB OFFER

Deans or those extending the offers to you should expect you to ask questions like the ones we just discussed. If they cannot answer your questions, they should be able to direct you to those who can. As we mentioned above, you may also choose to research whether the faculty have union representation. All colleges and universities don't have this, but it is worth determining. If there is a faculty union, you can receive valuable information about how to negotiate contracts on particular campuses. Unions can serve as wonderful reference librarians. They have answers to the research questions above. Unions will know the salary range in your prospective program and college. They can also tell you how the salary you have been offered compares to the university and what you should expect in your "employment package." Relocation and start-up research funds may be standard. They may not. Similarly, computers and 401K's may or may not be standard. In addition to letting you know if you are receiving an offer that is comparable to other in-coming faculty on the campus, unions cans advise you as to what you should ask for when you counter the offer.

You should still be able to receive negotiating assistance even if a union is not available. On most campuses, the role of the department or program chair hiring you is to assist you throughout the negotiation. Don't, however, initiate this conversation with the chair. If the chair offers to help you with the contract negotiation though, accept it. It is in the department's best interest to help you secure the best offer possible. On most campuses, then, your prospective chair will offer to speak to the dean on your behalf. In other words, when you counter the offer, you should expect help throughout this process. You want to make an informed decision. The schools should respect your attempts to do so.

To counter an offer, then, you want to do the following:

1. When an offer is extended, you should expect to receive it in writing. Do not accept an offer until it is in writing. During the phone call in which you receive the offer, think in terms of expressing your intentions. You can express your intentions without committing to the contract. If you receive a verbal offer from your first-choice school, you don't have to be cagey. You can let them know you want to join their faculty. Make sure you express your intentions without fully agreeing to the position:

   - "This is my first-choice school, and I look forward to seeing the contract."

   - "If the contract reflects the offer you've just outlined to me, I intend to accept it."

   - "Thank you so much for this offer. I look forward to reviewing the contract with my advisors/colleagues."

   Provisional answers like these allow the institution to make tentative plans to close their search. You may even get congratulatory emails and offers of moving help later the same day, as one contributor did.

2. Generally, you have two weeks to respond. Although a two week response time is considered professional etiquette, some schools will pressure you to make a decision sooner. The pressure is not usually mean-spirited. The search committee has likely created a short list of two candidates. If you don't accept the offer, the offer will go to the next candidate, and the committee doesn't want to lose the second candidate to another job while you decide. This may mean that you need to reach a compromise of, say, one week.

3. If you have received other offers or are anticipating others, let the dean (or person extending the offer) know. Doing so makes even clearer your reason for needing the two weeks to decide. You may be juggling several offers. Plus, schools like to know that other campus-

es are interested in hiring you. Knowing that you have received multiple offers can confirm a search committee's evaluation of you. Letting the dean know that you have other offers can be especially useful if you intend to ask for a higher in-coming salary.

4. When you receive an offer, it is polite to contact the other schools with whom you interviewed.

- You may be a top candidate on more than one campus.

Your phone call could be the impetus that forces a particular school to push the process along. Often financial forecasts delay the job offer process. A phone call that lets schools know other campuses are interested can force schools to make decisions.

- On the other hand, you may have a top-choice school that you hope is still considering your candidacy seriously.

Listen for the rhetorical clues in the department staff person's responses. (S)he probably has been instructed not to deluge the chair with phone calls from applicants, and furthermore legally cannot inform candidates of their status. Therefore, if you ask this staff person a question like, "Am I still being considered for the position?" be alert to the answers. One research university, for example, instructed its staff people to tell candidates no longer under consideration, "Ours is a very competitive institution." When the candidate rejoined, "I have another offer; should I hold out for word from you?" the staff person was instructed to repeat, "Ours is a very competitive institution." As an applicant, listen for these phrasings and repetitions. In this case, clearly the staff person has told you as clearly as (s)he can: Take the other position!

5. If you are part of an academic couple and the job offer will be feasible only if the school is able to offer your spouse or partner part-time work, let the dean know. Of course the challenge here is to determine when to inform the dean. We wish that we could answer with finality specific questions from academic couples, questions like:

- When would it be appropriate to disclose information about being part of an academic couple?

• Would it be useful for spouses to set up their own informational interviews after a candidate has been invited for an on-campus?

• Even for those couples who are not "academic couples," would it be useful for the spouse to accompany the candidate if for no other reason than to see if they could stand to live in a particular locale?

Although academic couples are not new to academe, as a profession, we have just begun to face directly the job search implications and realities for academic couples. Our colleagues are in the process of understanding how to best address this reality. As the authors of this book, we look forward to providing more specific advice in future editions of *Job Search*. At this point, we advise you to mention your academic couple status before the job offer is actually extended but not too early in the process. For instance, we don't encourage you to mention your academic couple status at the conference or first telephone interview. The only exception to this "rule" is if you know you will not be able to accept the offer unless your spouse or partner also gets some work. To mention your academic couple status at your discipline's conference is usually not wise. Doing so may halt conversations prematurely. To wait until the very end, though, may be read as presumptuous. Assistant Professor of Chemistry Jackie Trischman says, "Some schools are eager to show off how progressive they are in terms of partner benefits, maternity/paternity packages, and the like, but had to wait for the right questions from me." If these issues are important to you, be sure to give your interviewers openings to talk about them.

6. Review the offer closely in consultation with your dissertation committee, chair, or colleagues. Your committee or colleagues can be very helpful in clarifying the details of the offer and in helping articulate why you are countering the offer. As we mentioned in previous chapters, former classmates who already have faculty positions can also be especially helpful here. Your committee and colleagues may not have all of the answers, though. Dissertation committees want their students to get jobs, so while the committee can help you "read" the offer, the committee may not be as helpful in terms of explaining how to counter the offer. In fact, during

Dawn's negotiation stage one supportive mentor told her, "New Ph.D's have qualifications equivalent to those who went up for tenure a few years back. Those professors who have not been on the market recently, really don't know what it is demanding." This told Dawn that mentor comments were most likely dated. If the search committee offers to help you understand and negotiate your contract, accept this insider help. Dawn relied on advice from a search committee member who called her and said, "Counter this offer. Here's how," and from non-academic professionals who were skilled at countering offers. However, as we mentioned above, the union representative on the prospective campus is the person who should provide you with inside information about negotiating contracts on your campus.

7. Negotiate the details of your contract. Countering an offer is not greedy. You want to be certain that you will have resources such as adequate lab space, necessary computer components, and particular journal subscriptions you need to do your job. In Dawn's conversations with academics and non-academics, she was told that there is usually a little something campuses can do to make the job for which you're being hired just a bit more manageable. Negotiating may feel awkward, even tricky. Although you may feel as though you shouldn't counter, it is important to know that those extending the probably offer expect you to do so.

   Cheryl and Dawn advise you to negotiate these details in writing, making explicit the reconsideration you request. In other words, if you want a salary increase, be specific about how much of an increase you want and on what grounds. It is smartest to base that argument on your teaching or research history. Sometimes the teaching experience of new Ph.D.'s is ignored. Although the *vita* may show that you taught for three years at a community college with your Master's, this may have been overlooked when the offer was made. You want to point out kindly that you have three years of teaching experience in which you designed and taught classes. In other words, you were not "just" a teaching assistant. Or you may have extensive research experience outside of your dissertation research that should be translated again to the person extending the offer. Maybe you want an extension on the "dissertation in-hand clause" from, say, August 2000 to October 2000. Ask for this.

Those of you who are reluctant to counter offers, take heart: your counter offer may happen unknowingly or simply not be as explicit as a counter letter. During one contributor's campus interviews, for example, the interviewer explained that the school was interested in hiring her and named a particular salary. The candidate's eyes got big (she was happy with the offer.) The interviewer read her eye movement as a sign of slight disappointment and immediately raised the offer.

8. Be prepared for responses to your counter offer. When you counter an offer you usually expect responses from only the person who extended the offer. This may not be the case, though. Don't let that alarm you. The search committee is wanting you to accept the offer. They may not know that you are negotiating your contract. While the committee waits for your response, members may call you to see if there are questions that you have about the school or department. You may even be asked outright, "Are we your first choice? Who else is interested in you?" If you have competitive offers, it may be useful to mention that to the callers. These committee members usually chat with the department chair about these conversations. The chair may choose to use the information to request a revised contract from the Dean. You may or may not choose to answer the committee members' questions directly, though. That's ok. You are no longer the graduate student. And your interview process is over. Now you are trying to secure the best offer possible.

Responses to your negotiation process may not always be encouraging. Support from the chair is not always evident. One contributor who wishes to remain anonymous told us about a tricky contract negotiation. A search committee member advised the candidate to counter the offer by making explicit in a letter his teaching experience. The faculty member explained that the campus had a history of not reading new Ph.D.'s *vitae* carefully. The candidate submitted his counter offer after careful deliberation. His written response to the contract focused on his teaching and suggested a salary he thought was more commensurate with his experience. The chair responded to him by calling him to tell him "No one had ever done this [countered an offer] before." He insisted that all new Ph.D.'s came in at the bottom of the pay scale regardless of previous teaching experience. He explained that this was how the department maintained equity. The candidate accepted the salary offer being assured that the offer was equitable.

The story continued: once he was on the job, he was surprised to be told that union representatives' and other colleagues' research revealed that pay inequities existed. The result was that several years after being hired, he filed and received a salary adjustment. The process was laborious and revealing (the chair later explained that dealing with salary negotiations was new for him. He didn't know that faculty could counter offers).

The useful news for you is that with patience and persistence faculty grievance systems can work. We share this anecdote with you also so that you are aware that sometimes changes can be made once an offer is accepted. Work diligently though to make the first offer the best and most equitable it can be. Remember that it is perfectly appropriate to negotiate the initial offer. You want to. Although our anonymous contributor's situation was finally resolved, it took several years, and he will never recoup the money he didn't earn during those years. When it comes to academic contracts, schools can't make up to you what they don't offer initially.

9. Check the copy of the contract that you sign for any revisions. Often clerical errors unintentionally change dates in contracts. The first draft of one contributor's contract indicated that his dissertation was to be completed in April for a job that began the following September. The candidate, however, had promised during the interview process that the degree would be completed by June. When the candidate pointed out this small, but crazy-making change to the Dean, he nonchalantly extended the deadline to October.

The Rhetoric of Accepting or Rejecting a Job Offer

ACCEPTING THE OFFER

Accepting the offer is the simplest part of the process. Once you are satisfied with the offer, you simply sign the contract and return it by mail. It is not uncommon to send it both via fax and snail-mail. The fax assures the school of your decision, and the signature on the snail-mailed hard copy validates the agreement legally. In terms of the rhetoric of this stage, it is simple: you don't need to worry about the "messages" you might send by mailing it too early. You have used time to make your important decision. Once the decision is made, a quick response is acceptable.

REJECTING THE OFFER

The most frequent question regarding rejecting offers is "When should I do it?" If you know immediately that you will not accept an offer, even if the negotiating process is successful, let the school know. There are other candidates who will likely be extended the offer. The sooner you reply, the better chance the right candidate has of receiving the offer.

You may choose to reject an offer for a range of reasons:

- Your post-interview analysis of the position may convince you that it is not a good fit for you, your skills, and your personal obligations.
- You may receive other offers that are more attractive to you.
- You may have strong reservations about the one offer you receive.
- You may decide to accept a post-doc instead.
- You may decide that your dissertation will not be completed by the date promised. Or you may decide that you might receive even more competitive offers when you can interview with a completed dissertation.

Rejecting an offer can get complicated if you have one offer that needs a response in a week and you are expecting other offers. It will feel like a juggling act to you, and it will feel like a risky one at that. Even if you notify the other schools that you have received an offer, the timing doesn't always work out. One of our contributors told us,

I received a job offer from a school a half hour after I had been invited for a campus visit (and purchased a ticket) to the university that I really wanted to work at. Since the first school wanted an answer within a week, I had to find out where I stood at my first choice school and decide if I wanted to take the risk of rejecting a solid job offer. I ended up telling the first school that I couldn't give them an answer until a date that was about two weeks after the deadline they set. They let me know they would be making an offer to the next candidate. Luckily, it all worked out and the place I really wanted to work offered me the job at the end of my campus interview.

If you choose to reject an offer, know that you do not need to provide an explanation to the respective school. You can say very simply, "Thank you for the offer. I have, however, decided not to accept the offer." If you are turning down one offer for another or for a post-doc, you may say simply, "I have accepted another position." If an offer is especially low or offensive for some reason, it is wise not to mention that point when you reject the position. The person who extended an offer to you may move to another school in the future, one that is better funded, one that is therefore able to offer you a more impressive package. You may want to be a strong candidate for that position. The person who extended the offer to you will likely know deans on other campuses. You want to keep the lines of communication open.

The Rhetoric of Rejection

Rejection (never a good feeling) can come at different stages of the job search. Rejection after your discipline's conference interview usually comes in the form of a letter. The letters are typically quite generic. Rarely do the letters explain why you have not been selected for a campus interview (but maybe knowing that would only make you feel worse). The generic letters usually say, "The search for this position has been closed. Thank you for your application." If a rejection letter comes later in the search, it may mean that another candidate has been selected or that the department has been forced to end the search (in other words, the department may not be hiring anyone). The rejection then may have nothing to do with your credentials and everything to do with budgets. In the case where another candidate has been selected, you will likely prefer merely being told that another candidate has been selected. As impersonal as it seems, letters that try to say more usually end up offending candidates. In fact, more than one contributor told us that rejection letters which detailed the credentials of the new faculty hire sounded like braggadocio.

Rejections after the campus visit usually take one of two forms: the letter or the phone call. These letters tend to be more personal as the campus has met you. However, the school may still choose a generic letter in order to keep the process formal. At this stage, while the rejection phone call is common, it is also quite uncomfortable for both you and the person calling you. Remember, however, if you were invited to the campus, you were clearly one of the top faculty candidates. The campus has come to know you. To reject you is difficult. In one memorable rejection scenario, the chair of the Search Committee brought the candidate back to the airport and wished her well. Shaking her hand, the chair explained, "You interviewed very well. Don't change anything as you continue your interviews." The candidate was very encouraged by this. She'd done well!

A week later, when the chair called, there was an awkward silence after he gave his name. The candidate didn't know quite what to do, but the silence was deadly, so she responded by saying, "I assume you are calling to tell me something. It sounds like what you want to tell me is that you have extended the offer to someone else." Apologetically the man said, "Yes, I am sorry. Good luck to you." That was the end of the conversation. Like the staff person who repeated, "Our university is competitive," to candidates no longer under consideration, this chair's praise at the airport may have been a tacit acknowledgment that forces other than the candidate's credentials or interview performance were at play. The rejection call, then, was odd, but it does make clear how difficult these calls are on both sides. Search Committees want good things to happen for the faculty candidates they meet and are uncomfortable bearing bad news. Know that. Finally though the hiring committee has to make decisions based on their knowledge of you, of their college or university, and of their department. As Professor of Geography Jerry Pitzl told us,

> The point will be reached when the interviewers will come to a conclusion about whether or not the candidate would in fact be the "right" person to fill the slot. I characterize this point in the process as arriving at the answer to the question of proper "fit." Given the student clientele, the courses to be offered, and the need for the candidate to become a close colleague, will this person fit well into our department? Just as IBM or 3M or any other major corporation will attempt to find out how their applicants can significantly contribute to the corporate operation, the academic department must be assured that a candidate will fit well into their system. Define "fit"? That's up to the individual committee! This may seem too subjective; but it is essential (for the hiring department)!

Most importantly, should you experience rejection, remember the words of a contributor who is a faculty mentor and administrator at a large East Coast university. He insisted, "Tell THEM it's not THEIR fault."

How to Determine Whether a Second-Year Search is in Order

Before you decide whether to reinitiate the application-to-offer process the following year, you will want to think about the following:

- Now you have experience as a student and a faculty candidate. Do you still feel comfortable with academe?
- What are the academic job prospects like in your field?
- Do you still feel confident that you will find a job? If you are feeling defeated, it may show in future interviews for positions for which you are highly qualified.
- Do you feel confident that you will be able to find employment for another year while you continue your search?

If you feel confident about submitting applications once again, certainly do so. Before resubmitting your application though, look carefully at your application packet, paying careful attention to your teaching experience and your research interests. Also gather information about the strength of your letters of recommendation. One contributor's experience reveals how useful it can be to revisit your application packet. Assistant Professor of Sociology Alex Durig explains,

> It was the beginning of June 1994. I had three years of the job market under my belt. After three years though, I had done post-doc work, but I still didn't have a job. Then I had this sort of epiphany. I needed to "reinvent" myself. I had been marketing myself as a sociologist with expertise in social psychology and theory. These two sub-fields happened to be the least marketable. I thought carefully about my research skills and the research I had conducted. That afternoon, I decided that I would now market myself as a sociologist with health care and mental health (my field's hottest sub-fields). The next day, a professor visiting from West Coast University stopped by my office to

tell me his department was looking for a sociologist who studied health care and mental health. Within twenty-four hours after "reinventing" myself, I had a job! I had a job that later became a tenure-track position.

Durig's experience almost seems unreal, but it is a true story. Reidentifying and relabeling his skills made his fourth year on the market a success.

Durig's decision to relabel himself may have dissuaded future interviewers from reading his fourth year file with a bias. There appears to be an unfortunate bias against candidates who continue to throw themselves on an unforgiving market long after they've earned their Ph.D.'s. One of our colleagues, for example, spent several years after receiving his Ph.D. teaching at community colleges and teaching abroad. When he came back hoping this experience would have strengthened his candidacy, he found to his dismay that search committees looked askance at the time lag between the completed Ph.D. and his search for a "serious" job. If you find that you're going 'round and 'round the interview circuit, you may be too idealistic about finding the "right" academic job. You may, like our colleague, have experience that's difficult to translate in a profession that's geared to immediate advancement into a full-time position. You may even want to consider translating your skills for another profession entirely. This is not failure.

If you are beginning to imagine possibilities outside the academy, begin thinking about how you can translate your experience as a researcher, analytical thinker and writer, and teacher for the non-academic world. In fact, contributors who have made this transition often appear to utilize more of their skills than those of us who have entered tenure-track, "brass ring" positions.

If you are a skilled researcher,

- You are an independent thinker.
- You are able to follow necessary procedures.
- You are able to collect and sort information.
- You are able to ask critical questions and reach conclusions about information.
- You are resourceful; you know how to pull pieces of information together to solve problems.

If you are a successful teacher

- You know how to translate opaque concepts to other people.
- You know how to help others develop their critical thinking skills.
- You know how to facilitate discussions and evaluate performances.

These are valuable skills that private industry seeks. You may consider positions with publishing houses, with for-profit research companies, with corporate education programs, or with non-profit organizations. However, you will clearly need to translate your skills. As we discuss in chapter 6, an academic *vita* will confuse—not impress—the non-academic interviewer. You will find, however, that if you present yourself in a savvy way, the non-academic industry will likely show more respect for you than do your academic peers. (If you are contemplating a non-academic career, you may find the "Leaving Show-Biz" section in chapter 6 especially helpful).

Summary

- Remember that you can—and should— negotiate the details of your contract.
- The type of offer being made—tenure track, competitive tenure-track, non-tenure-track, or renewable—determines the negotiating power you have.
- Pay attention to your intuitive reactions to the entire interview process for a given position. Are you experiencing warning bells or just interview jitters?
- Read the rhetoric of the job contract closely.
- Follow professional etiquette when asking questions about the offer.
- Anticipate support—and static—through this negotiating process.
- Keep the needs of the institution in mind as you accept or reject offers.
- Remember that the rejection of your candidacy may have nothing to do with you, and everything to do with budgetary limitations or campus politics.

- If a particular search doesn't yield the job you want, reassess what you really want. It might be another year on the job market, or it might be an entirely different career from what you imagined.

6

RISING STARS
Academic and Nonacademic Success Stories

"A Star is Born": The Tenure-Track Professorship at the University

The interview process is the thoughtful act of constructing yourself. The whole process, in other words, helps you to see who you really are. Assistant Professor of Literature and Writing Studies Susie Lan Cassel told us, "I was constructing myself in the letters, in interviews. I entered this profession because I want to say what I truly believe." The process of finding a place from which to speak, in other words the interview process, says Lan Cassel, "is nothing if it not a search for self."

Embrace the job search as yours, not your mentors', your advisors', or even your partner's. You will certainly be guided by these people and their ideas—recall another contributor's advice to consider what a job might do to your living arrangements before you apply—but finally you have to speak for yourself. One assistant professor talks about the workshops her graduate institution offered: "In different workshops we talked a lot about finding a good fit. Revising my perception of what kind of a job I wanted allowed me to get a much better job than I expected." Another contributor explained to us that he had to step back from the professional label typically given to scholars doing the kind of work he does. He renamed himself.

He explains,

> It is ridiculous. In social psychology, which is where I was applying, a big research school would get 200 applications; smaller schools would get 100 or 120. It is brutal. I had to deal with this. So [now] I am a statistician. I am no longer a social psychologist. The number of applicants drops by about half for me with this label. I used another label, but I can still do my work. Being a statistician, I can do anything. I got what I was looking for.

A contributor who wishes to remain anonymous told us:

> I was extremely disappointed in my dissertation director because in September/October I asked for a letter of recommendation. She said, "No. I am sorry. I think it way too early to start your job search." I was her star student. We had a good working relationship. I had already sent out my applications. I thought I wouldn't get any interviews without a letter from my director. But not one person asked for that letter.

She had to go through the interview process without the support of her dissertation chair. Yet, she felt confident that she could have her dissertation done and that she was ready to be employed for the next academic year. This applicant received multiple offers the following spring and accepted a position at a state school where she is now an associate professor and chair of her program. You know when the time is right to start your search.

Repeatedly, tenure-track faculty who had been trained at research schools told us that one of the biggest challenges was justifying for themselves why they chose teaching schools over research institutions, especially when they had choices. Dissertation committees from these research schools usually applied a bit of pressure that made applicants feel that they were letting down their committees and not reaching their full potential as scholars. Assistant Professor of English Robert D. Sturr advises candidates to "see themselves as teaching professionals rather than as scholars." He told us,

> That sounds extreme, maybe, but I think it's true. Of course, I want to do research (and not just because of tenure). However, I honestly think I got my job because I could speak with the committee about the immediate and practical issues facing teachers at a community-based, mid-

western university. The interviews were the most exciting when I could point to specific examples from my teaching experience, and when pedagogy was discussed as both a theoretical and practical issue.

An associate professor adds her experience:

> In my training there was so little importance given to teaching, but on the market there was lots of importance given to teaching. Almost no one asked me detailed questions about my dissertation. A lot of them wanted know what I thought teaching goals should be. And this was across a broad range of schools: small liberal arts colleges up to Ph.D. granting institutions. Across the board, people were interested in teaching and in technology connected to teaching. In my program there were the academic stars or those interested in teaching. All of those interested in teaching got jobs right away.

Sturr encourages you to think about where you might be most happy. "You may even go into the interview as a student in one field, but then quickly find out that they want you to be more of a generalist." Remember that you are the one accepting the position and living with the job. This first position is where you begin constructing yourself as an employed professional. Let your job selection be an opportunity for you to celebrate what you value.

Know that even "stars" like the ones we've described here have their moments of self-doubt. A contributor who wishes to remain anonymous told us of his first experience reviewing faculty candidate files:

> I remember earlier this year looking at files for candidates and feeling completely inadequate. I suppose it's like a kid who gets a new, more exciting younger brother or sister. You feel like old meat. I looked at files (and, of course, I was still completely stressed out about finishing my dissertation!) and thought how good they looked. It was intimidating.

The Tenure-Track Professorship at the Community College

The community college interview experience is significantly different from that at the university. Although much of the advice in the previous chapters can be applied to either community college or university searches, the economic and institutional makeup of the community college sets up rhetorical situations at odds with university interview protocol. Many highly qualified candidates are, in fact, not taken seriously by community college search committees. Much of this has to do with the historical relationship between research universities and community colleges.

Research universities have traditionally looked at employment in the community college as far beneath the potential of any of their Ph.D. graduates. Many university mentors actively discourage graduates from applying to community colleges. As one assistant professor told us,

> I earned my Ph.D. from a major public research university which receives the bulk of public funding in our state. Faculty members were less than pleased when I decided to accept a tenure-line position at an urban community college in the same state.

Mentor elitism has led to several decades of abuse of the community college system: graduates who couldn't find jobs in their first-choice universities used the community colleges for "milk money" while continuing to look for more glamorous positions. Once hired at the community college, many of these applicants made pests of themselves by failing to embrace the community college's classroom mission and by failing to accept their colleagues as peers. Situations like these have become part of the lore of the community college system. Because of the historical lack of commitment by Ph.D.'s to the community college mission, then, today's Ph.D.'s have a tougher time convincing community college search committees (or even first-level application sorters) that they are, indeed, committed teachers.

Here are some things community college search committees worry about when they see a Ph.D. on your *vita:*

- Is this candidate truly committed to teaching? How can we know?

- Why has this candidate dedicated five or more years to intense research if (s)he truly wants a *teaching* position?

- Has this person absorbed the negative, competitive stance many research programs foster? Will (s)he want to be treated as a "star," never willing to function as part of the community?

- Does this candidate only think (s)he wants this job because the market is bad? Does (s)he realize what time constraints a 5-5 teaching load places on scholars?

- Will (s)he grow increasingly miserable when (s)he realizes how little time or funding (s)he'll have for research?

Community college search committee members are decidedly not anti-Ph.D. In fact, many community college teachers earn Ph.D.'s as part of their personal and professional development. Once you have a permanent position at the community college, the Ph.D. actually gains you extra earning potential. However, new Ph.D.'s who have no experience at the community college, and who suddenly appear among applicants who've taken less research-intensive training paths, set off all sorts of warning bells in a system that's been repeatedly abused.

One of our colleagues at a community college shares his own experience "on the other side of the desk" as an interviewer:

> Only a year after having been hired, I found myself on a hiring com-mittee enjoined to hire three new full time faculty. At the community college, at least on my campus, there still remain pockets of Ph.D. resistance. The prejudice comes across subtly and sometimes overt ly. In its most subtle form, it translates to lower scores on screening. During the interview process, it can come out as unrealistic expecta-tions for the candidate to perform more personably than other candi-dates (after all, Ph.D.'s aren't taught to teach—they are more inclined to research. If they want this job, they must be looking for something to fill in time before the job market opens up in the universities. Or better still, I've heard some say Ph.D.'s would just be bored teaching all the time).
>
> In its more overt form, prejudice against Ph.D.'s can come across disguised as an antagonism on the committee against theory. One can-didate I remember interviewing had some feminist theory presenta-tions on his or her *vita*. When this came up for discussion, the feeling among half of the group was that they could not work for the next twen-ty years with someone who will be stirring up trouble. Comments like these often lead to spirited discussions about the merits and demerits of theory.

Department chairs with whom we've worked in the community college tell us that, if you have a Ph.D. and want to teach at the community college, it is best to interview for an adjunct position first—preferably before you receive the Ph.D. Once the faculty recognizes that you are a team player and that your primary focus is teaching, the possibility of a permanent teaching position is much more real. Both authors have experienced this first-hand in working for community colleges. Dawn, for example, started working in a community college writing center while she was completing her Ph.D. Cheryl began teaching as an adjunct as soon as she was ABD. At the M.A. level, neither author had difficulty in securing these part-time jobs. When Cheryl obtained her Ph.D. and applied for full-time positions at some thirty community colleges, however, the only invitations she received to pursue community college positions came from the campuses at which she had worked as an adjunct. One of our doctorate-laden contributors—who later accepted a position at a major Midwestern university that is renowned for its experimental, innovative teaching focus—likewise received no callbacks from any of the community colleges to which she applied.

The community college, then, is not a "fall back" position for applicants uncertain they can obtain a more research-oriented position. Neither is the community college job search a university job search. Candidates who apply for community college interviews are selecting teaching and community service as their primary foci. These candidates may be interested in some research, but they know that the community colleges will rarely provide research funds to make specific projects possible or to travel to professional conferences. In fact, community college faculty who choose to present at disciplinary conferences may have to pay their own way and will have to find a substitute to cover class in their absence. Since adjunct faculty are paid only for their classroom hours, if they present at conferences, their time away from the classroom is docked from their paychecks.

Further, the search is no less demanding (and in some cases more demanding) than a university search. Assistant Professor of History Tandy McConnell's experience makes the point clear:

> My first interview was at a local community/technical college. The interview went great. The other guy—who had already been teaching there—got the job. The chair of the humanities department asked me if I would like to teach as an adjunct. I took it.
>
> In January I was contacted by another community college for an interview. Again the interview went well. A month later I called to discover that the position had been filled and that I would not be receiving any compensation for travel.

In February I was contacted again by a state school. Could I fly up for an interview in a week? Of course! This interview was grueling, but seemed to go well also. I was the first of three interviewees. I returned home.

The community college interview clearly requires persistence in order to reap rewards. McConnell was finally offered a position after a rather long audition:

> I have been working this semester as a full-time adjunct. I have taught occasional classes for them, and when a senior faculty member retired, I was asked to fill in during the search for his replacement. I applied feeling that, if the college hired someone else, I would give up on academic life, even though I felt it to be my calling and bliss. Well over one hundred people applied for the position. I was offered the position on the day after I returned from [an]other interview. The position was not wired and was not a sure bet. Rather, I was on a semester-long job interview, and all of the candidates were considered.

Because of its intense focus on the student, however, community college teaching can be one of the most rewarding faculty positions you encounter. One former community college professor, now an assistant professor at a state college, told us of her mixed reactions to her years at the two-year college:

> Teaching at the community college was one of the most moving experiences I have ever been privileged to take part in. At the same time, it was a very difficult situation: the lowest salaries in the region; extremely limited access to library facilities, technology, and funding for conference attendance and research; and precious little time to write.

One of our former graduate classmates (who, by the way, makes several thousand dollars *more* at the community college than those of us who took on university positions) once mused that the community college's de-emphasis on research can actually be a boon. Not only does it mean less stress as you wait for feedback from publishers and editors, but publications are often treated as occasions to celebrate. While the response to publication at the research university is often, "So, what else are you doing?," at the community college, he told us, "They give you a faculty reception and tea."

One colleague at a community college emphasized these points about the community college search:

> The two most important points that kept coming up repeatedly were these: the committee wanted, above all, a teacher and they wanted someone with whom they thought they could work for the next twenty years. It's pretty clear that neither of these can be measured in an interview, and only one can be measured in less than twenty years. Be that as it may, the committee at least wanted to hear that so-and-so was a good teacher because so-and-so loved, thrived in, and excelled in the classroom.
>
> When asked, "What makes you a good teacher," too many candidates answered that they were good teachers because their students loved them and they were rough/fair/easy on the students. Few, if any, replied that they were good teachers because, by God, they could teach. That's what they want to do and that's all they want to do. Teaching is life. Teaching, teaching, teaching. As a committee, we were very concerned that that be the primary mission of each candidate.

If you have a Ph.D. and are interested in finding a secure job at a community college, know that you will need to make even more clear than an M.A.-bearing applicant your reasons for applying to the school. Consider how you can contextualize your Ph.D. for the community college campus. Your community college interview will focus on teaching, just as your community career will. To prepare fully for the community college interview, this colleague strongly advises:

> Use the rhetorical skills you've been taught. Read the job announcement carefully, research the institution you are being interviewed by, consider the audience and what message would be most appropriate to that audience. The goal here is to get a job; all of your skills should be harnessed to that effort.

"Most Original Character": The Nontraditional Job Search

Success in the job search doesn't result from formulaic approaches to the market. The traditional *vita,* to conference interview, to on-campus interview trajectory may not be possible immediately after graduate school—or you may even find that your talents and interests are so diverse you need to create your own job niche. Here, two of our contributors tell us how non-traditional approaches to the job market gained them valuable experience and ultimately jobs they could live with.

GREG BEATTY, ONLINE EDUCATOR

Having looked at what I want to do with my life, and what academia offers, I am, for now, choosing to opt out of the far too familiar frenzied search for that good tenure-track job. My partner has a tenure-track job at a mid-sized state university—quite a good job in this market—and spends more time advising, attending committee meetings, and doing paperwork than I can imagine stomaching. I also don't see most of those activities furthering teaching.

I like to write and to think. My interests are too varied for me to be at ease in most positions, and my writing interests include fiction. Here too, I want to be able to work by my own standards, not churn out articles that no one will read. If I am to be a writer and scholar, I want to write things I'm proud of, in all of my areas of interest: genre fiction, early-American lit and culture, critical theory, alternative communities, theorizing the body, etc. I tend to think that many intellectual and moral battles can be carried out better in the public sphere than within academia. This means writing editorials, book reviews—and perhaps comic books.

Beatty's job search reflects these personal values; ironically, his partner's success in inhabiting a tenure-track position spurred him to seek more flexible options:

My partner got a job in another state. She moved there. We spent a year apart and missed each other. I wanted to be near her. I spent a lot of time working through my possibilities and desires in traditional academia, and decided that I wanted to carve my own path. Time will tell if this was a foolish judgment, but the first year has been exhilarating; most of the best things have come as a result of need (of money) and curiosity.

By carving his own path in an emerging field, Beatty gained not only geographical flexibility, but the intellectual freedom usually associated with a tenure-track position at a research university. After hearing about an opening with an online school from a friend, he submitted a *vita* and application letter. His interviews came via a surprise telephone call.

> A couple weeks after I sent in my c.v., Beatty relates, I got a phone call from a faculty recruiter at Electronic College, who wanted to interview me then and there. As we stumbled our way through an interview for which I was totally unprepared, the recruiter mentioned, quite in passing, that my c.v. showed "an incredibly wide bandwidth," and that, in his experience, was the sort of person who did well teaching online.

Beatty's "on-campus presentation" was a brief online training course, followed by a teaching evaluation and his formal hire:

> Each school requires at least 6 weeks of training—study, observed teaching, exercises, and the like—and requires would-be faculty to observe at least one full class before teaching, to assure an in-depth understanding of how an online class should be taught. After that, I was observed by an experienced teacher for a test class. Only after that time was I considered a faculty member. Roughly 25 percent of those accepted for training fail or leave voluntarily; another 10 percent leave after or during the test class.

Teaching online has had some unexpected professional benefits for Beatty, who tells us, "As a result of my online teaching experience I have also found myself, quite by accident, at the relative forefront of technological changes. My partner's school is holding meetings about putting classes online; I visit as a local expert." Rather than looking at this unconventional teaching job as something "less-than" the brass ring held out for graduating Ph.D.'s, Beatty cites many advantages to teaching online:

> I can have a flexible schedule. I teach in the morning, at night, or whenever I get to the machine. I also repeat classes again and again, which lets me get good at them. Almost without exception, online learners choose to be there. I don't have to fight any surly, "why should I care" freshmen. Finally, I am bringing education to the backcountry and retraining single moms, all of which is more in line with my politics and personal values than most educational situations. The money allows me to live with my partner; the flexible schedule allows me to

practice tai chi and do my own writing, and do all the cooking for my household.

My current academic employment allows me to put my own values first. Since these are not traditional values, this has not been a traditional track. However, by embracing the nontraditional, I have found that I am converting the involuntary situation of marginal employment many recent graduates encounter into a relatively voluntary position.

JEANNE-MARIE ZECK, VISITING ASSISTANT PROFESSOR OF ENGLISH

Jeanne-Marie Zeck used a visiting professor position "to acquire new skills and hone new areas of expertise." She found that filling holes in her host institution's schedule added to her own marketable skills, allowed her to teach her passions, and opened up research opportunities:

> Teaching independent studies prepared me for teaching a survey that covered 230 years of literature. Now in my letters of application for tenure-track jobs I can describe the courses I have taught in African American Literature [courses she designed for an independent study student] rather than simply stating that African American Literature is an interest of mine. Since that first experience I've taught two more classes: Asian American Authors and Native American Authors. Both classes were wonderful; the students learned a lot and so did I. The Native American course led to my own summer-long research project on Michael Dorris which I have since submitted for publication. Independent studies can be great opportunities to satisfy students' needs and to teach exactly what I'm interested in and improve my expertise.

Independent studies courses allowed her the autonomy of designing her own courses, a skill highly prized by search committees inundated by applications from marvelous new graduates who have only taught other people's courses as teaching assistants. However, there was a price to pay for this autonomy. Zeck tells us, "One thing I quickly learned regarding independent studies is that they require a huge amount of work, even if there is only one student. Since teaching those first two classes, I've learned to only say 'yes' to independent studies for very motivated students."

Another benefit that Zeck found in her visiting professorship (one which job seekers in the "dialectic" mode would interpret as exploitation) was committee work and community service:

> While at State University I've been very involved with committee work and advising students on their honors papers. Through these activities I earned quite a good reputation on campus. One of my colleagues who noticed the attention I gave my honors' students (I always come to the class sessions when they present their papers to their peers), asked me to be on the academic standing committee. This committee is both an important job and a job that requires little time (an unusual combination). On this committee, I am able to offer information on particular students I've had in classes. I also am able to interact with other professors from various departments.
>
> One thing I discovered is that the more I got involved with campus life, the more I enjoyed my work, my students, and my colleagues. One of my favorite activities at State University is the faculty seminars. In the Spring a group of interested folks meets and decides on six books that will be offered to faculty and staff for the following year, three in the Fall and three in the Spring. This is a book club that is just for the sheer pleasure of reading and discussing books with colleagues. Each year I've been involved as a both a discussion facilitator and a host. I enjoy having people to my house and this is a great way to increase my number of acquaintances. These activities really make me feel like a part of the State University community and they remind me that there is more to work than work!

Zeck's visiting position also allowed her to become familiar with typical university bureaucracy—experience that will give her interview sessions for permanent positions a ring of insider knowledge unusual in entry-level faculty applicants:

> Another of my greatest pleasures is taking the students on trips. This requires learning about bureaucratic red tape and university policies. Once I figured out how to plan a trip and fund it, I began offering a lot of them. Again, I earned a reputation as a professor who cares about the students very much. So much that I'm willing to use weekend time to take Women's Studies students to Seneca Falls, NY, to visit the site of the first women's convention in the U.S., and [to take] literature students

to all ends of the earth for poetry readings by Tess Gallagher and Li-Young Lee and Joy Harjo. I've also taken students to Washington D.C. to see Maya Lin's Vietnam Veterans Memorial and the National Museum of Women in the Arts. And I've taken students to see professional theater productions. These trips tend to strengthen bonds among the students and between the professor and the students. They are a real source of pleasure. (I've also become quite an expert at driving those gigantic vans!)

Zeck advises people who take visiting professorships to take advantage of—and create—opportunities for their own development via the resources available on their temporary campuses.

Another advantage of a visiting professor position is that there will probably be professional development money available. If it isn't offered, ask your colleagues, department heads, and deans. Chances are, there is a fund available. During your "visit," keep your professional life moving forward. I've used my summers and breaks for research and each year I've attended a conference and published at least one article.

Also, take advantage of the opportunities right on your campus to improve your teaching. Attend workshops offered for faculty members; visit the classrooms of your colleagues and ask them to visit yours. While here at State University I organized, and continue to manage, a departmental project that I call "Faculty Research Gatherings." Three times each semester the English department faculty gather at someone's house. The host provides a main dish for dinner and others bring side dishes and desserts. After relaxing over the potluck meal and conversation, a department member informally presents her or his current research. This has proven to be a real highlight of our academic year. We get to know each other well and discover what each person is currently researching. Also, when research questions and problems arise, the gathering is a great opportunity to offer one another help. These gatherings are another reminder that our work should be and can be a joyful experience.

"Leaving Show-Biz": Jobs Outside of the Academy

Although the tenure-track faculty position at a research university is the ultimate goal most graduate students are taught to work towards, many emerging scholars are finding that none of the career paths available to them in the academy are satisfactory. They brave a very strongly ingrained bias against non-academic employment in order to seek careers outside the academy. Let's meet a few of these "characters."

One contributor who wishes to remain anonymous commented:

> If academics don't want or can't use my talents, then I'll take them where they are wanted and can be used to do some good. I'm exhausted running into brick walls in the academy." And another told us, "I am presently in a nontenure-track position. Upon receipt of my degree [Ph.D.], I was promoted to assistant professor, but there is still little hope of this becoming a tenure-track position. *Thus,* I am taking a big look at the whole profession, flirting with getting out of it, and trying to understand the whole tenure/job search game.

Despite their willingness to go another route, many new Ph.D.'s find that the advanced degree can put you into a bracket in which the jobs you did to get through graduate school are no longer appropriate. Assistant Professor of English Marcy Tanter's experience is common:

> I have learned that a Ph.D. isn't very useful outside academia and that my English department was not very good at preparing me for life outside academia. I am either constantly being told I'm overqualified or simply don't get interviews for jobs like administrative assistant, proofreader, library assistant. No one believes that I would possibly want to do something else with my degree. It's very frustrating.

While exploring alternatives to the tenure-track position, Cheryl interviewed for management consultant positions. The fresh-faced, navy blue-suited interview teams weren't sure what to make of her in an applicant pool awash with new BA's. Achieving the Ph.D. means that you have been inhabiting and co-creating the academy for quite a large chunk of years. Have you overeducated yourself? Made yourself an "ugly duckling," with no swan families available for adoption? Is there a basic incommensurability between the academy and the world outside the ivory tower? Many contributors have found (or created) bridges leading out of the academy, finding the task to be one of construction and translation.

If you decide or are forced to think about leaving the academy, you have to change the way you think about what jobs you can do. Before you start sending your standard faculty application packet to employers outside the academy, consider how you might translate your experience and training in ways that business people will understand. The focus of the world outside academia is quite different from that which you've been immersed in during graduate school, but you can sell your abilities as a real coup for the hirer if you work your search with savvy. Since graduate school prepares you to work hard intellectually in an operation largely geared to service, think about the possibility of starting a service-oriented business of your own—or even working in a staff position within the academic community, as has Amanda Taylor, a Ph.D. student soon to graduate from an East Coast University.

AMANDA TAYLOR: THE UNIVERSITY STAFF POSITION

Taylor muses, "It seems that whenever people talk about nonacademic work, we usually think of the corporate world. Staff positions at universities are somewhere between academia and corporate culture. The first thing I think worth pointing out, is that such jobs exist." Taylor has worked in University staff positions throughout her graduate years: "I've worked as a writer/editor at the Institute for the study of adult literacy, as a thesis editor in the graduate school, and, in my current position, as writer/editor-admissions counselor in the undergraduate admissions office."

Thus, she feels none of the abject terror many students seem to suffer when they consider alternatives to the tenure-track position:

> I'm now in a position to say that if the job market doesn't work out for me, I have a lot of marketable skills and I know what kind of jobs I could look for, and how to move ahead in them. Perhaps more importantly, working in a staff position has nurtured my self-confidence and my social skills. University staff members (though some would disagree with me) by and large work together and work in teams much better than faculty. I experience a much greater sense that my colleagues in my office respect me and that my opinion counts. My tasks are real, not "practice" for some distant future when I've been fully credentialed.

For Taylor, working as part of the university staff has already drawn her into participation in the working "dialogic" we discussed in our introduction. This allows her to inhabit productively her transitional status as colleague-in-training:

I feel that some of the dimensions of graduate school that result from the student's sense of being still in training (which certainly we are) can be demoralizing, and that one of the benefits of a staff job for me has been to offset some of the feelings of inadequacy that being in training throughout your twenties can induce. As a scholar, I'm still in training, but there are important things that I'm already capable of doing, and my job proves that to me on a daily basis.

If you decide to seek jobs outside the academy, scour the trade publications listed in our appendix 5 for hints about how to present yourself in realms that speak a different rhetoric from the academy. Despite its increasing implementation of corporate models, the academy remains focused on issues other than the "bottom line," and the value it assigns particular characteristics, desires, and attitudes can make discussions with corporate interviewers seem like you've dropped into an alternate universe. Yet, the skills you develop in your graduate years can be highly prized outside the academy. Your task is to package your candidacy in language that makes sense in nonacademic settings.

Luckily, a whole industry of trade guides exists to address job hunting in the business realm. Most often, these guides can be obtained free of charge from the public library, and some universities have solid holdings in this genre as well. Use these guides to get a feel for the language used in business and the priorities set on particular skills, training, and experience. You don't have to change who you are and what you want to do in order to get a job outside of the academy. You do have to reformulate a professional persona that can inhabit a whole new set of job descriptions. Give some thought, then, to how your goals, values, and expertise can be recontextualized so that they become "legible" in the world of work.

In fact, despite their apparent success in securing tenure-track jobs, many professors fantasize about becoming editors or starting their own publishing houses. One editor, who left academe for a large publishing house, told us that the things she really valued in academe—research, connecting people with ideas—were prerequisites for a successful publishing career. Because most graduate schools make those who choose alternatives to the tenure-track professorship feel guilty and inadequate, she had to step back and realize that she could enjoy a publishing career for the same reasons she imagined she would enjoy a career in teaching and research. One former editor, in fact, *left publishing* to become a teacher at a two-year college. The two fields in many ways mirror each other. Another editor cautioned us, however, that academics have to learn to present themselves, their training, and their experience for a broader audience, one focused on profit as well as enlightenment.

DONNA REISS—PUBLISH OR PERISH WITHOUT PAY: AN ALTERNATIVE TO ACADEMIA

This final vignette shares Associate Professor of English Donna Reiss's decision to complete her advanced degree, leave academia, and return to it as a professor twenty years later. Our hope is that her experience can help you imagine how your academic training and nonacademic experience might benefit you in your professional life.

* * *

Despite having spent several years struggling for a degree in hopes of finding a dream job in the professoriate, graduate students and recent graduates won't be wasting their time or their energy by writing for free. How better to learn to teach audience and purpose than to write for a variety of audiences and purposes as a volunteer? Where will you get the grant-writing experience that will buy you time for additional research in the future unless you write—and receive—grants for agencies as a public service?

What I did for fun beginning with captions for the high school yearbook turned eventually into a diverse portfolio demonstrating that I was a "writer" and "editor." My training ground was less my classes than my extracurricular activities. In college, I was an unpaid copy editor for the newspaper and co-author of the class play. After college during a period when I was not working full time (and before I knew about part-time teaching as a career option), I wrote for clubs and organizations that were of interest to me. I volunteered to do their press releases—and thus learned how to write press releases. I wrote letters to the editor and to members of Congress that were signed by the club officials (not by me) that gave me the confidence eventually to write my own authentic arguments. I edited their newsletters. I wrote their grant proposals. I even spoke on their behalf to television reporters. And I gained experience that helped me do the same work professionally years later.

A regional magazine was my first paid publication. My small portfolio of clippings earned me a chance to try a short piece. Eventually, I was writing human-interest columns and features, personality profiles that gave me experience conducting interviews and turning pages of notes into portraits of other people's lives. I was willing to write about almost anything, including business ventures, medical issues, travel, and one of my favorites, a story about local golf courses, a favorite because although I don't play or like golf (but adore the phrase "a good walk spoiled"), I did like the challenge of the topic. I visited all of the courses and talked to all the pros and then teamed with an artist to illustrate the article with an idealized course of the best holes in the area.

Meeting deadlines and working well with editors were my strongest skills. Without a single course in journalism, I became a journalist. Eventually I was able to expand my repertoire to working with writers as an editor for a small regional publishing company that I cofounded, and that still exists with new owners. At a small struggling business, everybody does everything, so I wrote dust jacket copy, promotional brochures, and catalog copy. I dealt with writers, typesetters, graphic artists, printers, and booksellers. I edited books. I did some layout and paste-up. I packed books and carried the boxes to the post office. I did everything except the accounts (my partners knew I had no facility with numbers; but truth be told, if they'd needed me to keep the books, I probably would have).

When I left that business, I entered another freelance career that allowed me to combine my passion for cooking and dining with the pleasure and small profit of writing a regular column as a restaurant critic and restaurant news columnist (Yes, they paid me and "my dinner companions" to eat). And as a writer and editor I first came to appreciate the computer, a tool that encouraged and facilitated revision and permitted the preservation of multiple shareable drafts. When my editor asked me to submit my copy electronically, I bought a modem and was on my way to my current work in higher education, teaching classes enhanced by computers or delivered on-line and consulting with other teachers on how to do the same.

The "volunteer" period and the meagerly paid experience of my young adulthood provided superb training for my academic career of the last decade. That background helps me write grant proposals for myself, my department, and my college. Public relations practice helps me gather support and publicity for a variety of projects, and working with graphic designers gives me at least a superficial sense of layout and space that has influenced my homemade fliers and web pages. That decade away from the academy helped me to appreciate it more when I came back to teaching, and I recommend a similar detour for other English majors not immediately able to step into college or university positions.

I've never earned my living entirely as a freelance writer and editor; however, I know from several people who do so that it is possible. There's a certain relentless hustling for work in a capricious market that never fully appealed to me, but had I not had the good luck to be teaching (first part time and now full time) I probably would have learned those skills as well. So the very situation that kept me away from the classroom twenty years ago—moving to a new community and unable to find a teaching job—led me to wonderful opportunities to become a writer and editor and prepared me well for teaching undergraduate writing and literature. I became an advocate for communication across the curriculum and explored the pedagogical possibilities of new media.

* * *

Academic and nonacademic success stories abound. Our hope is that by reading the real experiences of professionals like you who have earned advanced academic degrees, that you will be encouraged to imagine the exciting range of professional positions you can pursue. Most importantly, you should not feel that advanced degrees in research limit you to academic positions. Instead, learn to translate your professional skills, interests, and values for both the academic and nonacademic worlds. Should you choose to pursue positions outside of the academy, you will find the professionals there especially appreciative of your skills.

The Director's Chair: Being an Ethical Academic

I have seen how very out of touch most job search advice is. . . .
[C]oncrete advice is seriously out of date.

—On-line Educator Greg Beatty

My job search has been a nightmare. It has been so bad, that my story
is the one graduate students scare each other with around the camp-
fire at night.

Job Seeker

Once you are employed (i.e. in the director's chair), you can influence the
politics and ethics of the job search. In this final section, we encourage new
academic hires along with their senior colleagues to use their understanding
of the job market to make search and hiring practices more professional and
equitable. Contributors to *Job Search* kindly shared helpful coaching tips and
awkward but potentially avoidable experiences. These suggestions represent
a call for faculty to look closely at how they prepare their graduate students
for the job market and how universities interview candidates. Reviewing faculty candidates' experience-based requests will surely help you conduct fair-
er interviews that only benefit academe.

1. Prepare Graduate Students Intentionally for the Job Search

The answers to how to be successful on the job market don't need to be hidden. Be proactive faculty mentors. Several universities have already established departmental systems and workshops geared towards preparing students for the interview process. If your new department hasn't yet organized its professional guidance for graduate students or if professional training programs need to be redesigned, you will appreciate hearing contributors' comments about the guidance that worked:

- Graduate programs can secure grants geared towards training students for the job search. One assistant professor explains that this money is then used

    1. To design sequenced workshops on creating a *vita,* building a teaching portfolio, reading job ads, interviewing at the conference and campus, and being a first-year faculty member.

    2. To professionalize graduate students and to educate graduate students about the state of the profession.

- Graduate departments can appoint faculty to prepare graduate students for the job search. The appointed faculty can then treat the job search as a part of the graduate curriculum by providing useful materials, mock interviews, and more. This approach worked well for Assistant Professor of Literature and Writing Studies Susie Lan Cassel and others. She suggests that the appointed faculty member guide applicants through the process by doing the following:

    1. Providing useful tools and assistance like

        a. Packets of information that include interview strategies, cover letters, and *vitae* from the junior faculty who were recently hired into the department. These samples allow applicants to imitate successful rhetorical strategies.

        b. Mock interviews with critical feedback. Cassel explained that mock interviews followed by debriefing sessions were especially useful, for they make clear what we had done well and what the interviewees would likely expect to hear. The mock interviews help you "learn to read through the questions."

 c. Dossier assistance. The appointed faculty member can help applicants both create and mail these professional portfolios. Some universities' dossier mailing services are separate from graduate students' home programs. If the appointed faculty keeps copies of applicants' dossiers, he can usually respond more quickly to interviewing colleges and universities requests for confidential dossiers.

 d. Support at the conference interview.

2. Keeping other faculty informed of applicants' interview progress so that fellow faculty can also extend assistance. Faculty want to help. They just need a mechanism for knowing which applicants might benefit from their assistance.

3. Organizing forums at which former graduate students discuss their experiences on the job market with those students new to the market. The forum should include graduates who have academic and non-academic careers.

• Graduate programs should create job placement data bases. As graduate student Patrick McCord explains, this data lets departments know how well their students do on the market and benefits future applicants.

• Graduate students and faculty may organize themselves into small job-search coaching groups. Assistant Professor of Psychology Gina Grimshaw told us,

My program put a lot emphasis on graduates getting jobs. We had thirteen to fifteen students in our graduate program at any one time. The group ranged from first to sixth year students. Each person went through the interview-practice process of everyone before us—the job talks and all. The students and all faculty attended.

• If the graduate program can't provide the support, individual faculty members can. Associate Professor of Management Regina

Eisenbach recalled that her mentor did the following:

1. sent out letters on her behalf introducing her to colleagues
2. coached her on her *vita* and cover letter

• If faculty don't provide job search support, graduate students may organize themselves. In fact, Casie Hermansson and Margaret McGeachy designed an extensive workshop to prepare their peers for the market (see appendix 3).

In addition to departmental assistance, your university may provide job interview preparation workshops through the Career Center, Faculty Development Office, or Graduate School. Your university may also have an affiliation with the Preparing Future Faculty program. Any or all of these resources may benefit your students as you prepare them for the job market. However your program prepares graduate students for the profession, aim for a thoughtfully designed program. It shouldn't be an accident that students are prepared for the job market. Graduate programs should introduce students to the profession by preparing them for their job searches.

2. Design Professionally Respectable Interview Itineraries

You want to keep this in mind at both the conference and campus interviews. Several contributors commented that they found it odd that interviewers scheduled candidates back to back. The interviewers wondered whether search committees were taking them seriously. Could search committees be serious about the interview process if they gave themselves no time to debrief before another interview began? Furthermore, one contributor reminds committees,

Scheduling candidates one right after another, without time to differentiate them in your mind or take notes on them may seem efficient to you. It may even seem professional not to keep the next candidate waiting at the cattle call, but actually it doesn't give search committee members time to separate each candidate from the others, to discuss the interview that just happened, or even to take notes on impressions.

Schedule debriefing time into your interview conference interviews. You will appreciate this. To allow for this post-interview discussion period simply schedule ten minutes of time after each interview. In other words, if each interview is scheduled to run thirty minutes, allow thirty minutes for the interview and ten minutes for the debriefing session. During these debriefing sessions, discuss and record the search committee's comments about the candidate. These brief notes will help the committee recall the details of the interview at a later time.

For the campus interviews, Cheryl encourages search committees to build in free time for candidates to relax and think away from the committee. Cheryl explains her experience as part of one search committee:

The search chair was worried about letting a candidate drive alone to a restaurant where we were all meeting. He was looking at it as courtly attention, but I said, "Candidates have so many people to meet and so many different presentations of themselves to make on the campus visit that they need some space in which to mull it all over. She'll probably enjoy her 15 minutes alone in the car."

Recall that at campuses with overpacked schedules, the bathroom became Dawn's sanctuary—her private place to pause and prepare for upcoming interviews. If you keep the interview schedules realistic for both the search committee and the candidate, all of you will be happier. Promise.

3. Tell the Truth about the Job

Associate Professor Michael Day encourages you to remember that faculty candidates like to gather specific information about the status of the job. They also like to know what the job will involve. He advises the following:

• Tell applicants up front if the position is contingent on as-yet unsecured funding.

• Make very clear what the job entails. Don't lure someone in with talk of electives and specific classes if you know you can't really offer the new hire those classes.

- Be clear about what committee and advising duties the new hire will have. Day recounts, "That was a big shock for me. I spend a great deal of time calculating transfer credits, doing degree checks, and meeting with and chairing various campus committees."

- Let the candidate know how and in what categories Internet discussion groups and web publications will count toward tenure and promotion, if they count at all.

The more honest and direct you are with candidates about what the job really entails, the better chance you have of hiring faculty who will stay at your campus for a significant amount of time.

4. Craft Ethically and Legally Sound Interview Questions.

Recall from chapter 4 that some search committees blatantly ask questions about age, ethnicity, class, gender, and sexuality while other committees' unethical questions are less obvious—and possibly more insidious. To ask explicit questions like those below is illegal and wrong:

- *What is your race?*

- *What is your ethnicity?*

- *Where is your mother from?*

- *What kind of birth control do you use?*

- *How old are you?*

Equally insensitive are questions like:

- *What brought you to African American studies?*

- *What brought you, you personally, to African American studies?*

- *Where did you learn Chinese?*

- *Is this your married name?*

Not only are the questions illegal, they move the interview away from one that focuses on credentials to one that appears to be all about selling personal histories. Remember that your focus at interviews is on credentials, not personal lives.

Assistant Professor of English Ellen M. Gil-Gomez's "The Ghosts in the Machine: Women of Color and the Job Market" makes clear search committees' ethical obligation to recognize the questions they ask. Significant excerpts from Gil-Gomez's article are included below.

ELLEN M. GIL-GOMEZ, ASSISTANT PROFESSOR OF ENGLISH—
EXCERPTS FROM "THE GHOSTS IN THE MACHINE: WOMEN OF
COLOR AND THE JOB MARKET"

Clearly it's the interview setting that is most ripe for an examination of power. It's common knowledge on the interview scene that female candidates are sometimes treated differently than male candidates.

. . .

If we consider that there is a connection between the interpretation of a candidate's identity and the identity of the interviewer, along with the fact that the majority of professors in all disciplines is white, it's likely that women of color will be judged by white interviewers. How does this situation affect candidates who are women of color?

. . .

At the time [of my job search], I had no real idea how to deal with these questions. Sometimes they were asked in earnest and others in uncomfortable jest. I had not been prepared to encounter these kinds of questions and clearly they were ones that I could not answer well as trap doors that seemed to loom no matter where I looked. A significant question to ask was the following: How do I size up this person's view of me as a "person of color" based on the question? Besides the obvious problems of sizing anyone for anything is the question of who is being represented by this phrase "person of color." Going through my mind were all of the options I might choose to construct: Should I be "upitty," "authentic and exotic," "pulled up by the bootstraps," "grateful for a chance," "political," "compassionate to liberals," "white washed"? These were all descriptions I'd been given as an academic in my own education and as a candidate. Running simultaneously along with these so-called options was my concern with constructing any of these identities in direct response to how I felt an interviewer might be leading me. I was not only one candidate here but a whole category of persons depending on whom the interviewer saw in me and my materials.

. . .

After one year on the market, the whole meta-discourse of job ads suddenly dominated my thinking. I started to see the whole event of searching for a job as a performative construction of my identity. At the time I hadn't realized that the interviewers and committee members were trying to construct an identity for me; but not an identity based on courses taught and papers given. Only afterwards was it apparent that these white professors were trying to "get" a minority for the various positions but they wanted to make sure the person was the right kind of minority—this meant that I had to fit into their fabricated stereotype of what an Hispanic was. No one ever wondered, apparently, if I was Mexican or not. Since I was from California, I guess I was by default. After realizing this, I clearly saw the white supremacy, sexism, and classism that informed many of these uncomfortable moments and questions. But why was this never a topic of discussion at these mock interviews and job seminars? It clearly was an important factor in all of my interviews. After remaining unemployed after this first year's search, I became obsessed with deconstructing everything.

. . .

It's ugly and it's true that the institution itself is created in a way to intentionally keep minorities out; to intentionally keep power structures intact. I was being told that I would automatically succeed, and on the other hand being given no support and was in fact being punished and given less support. I was angry that I was receiving the "wonderful benefit" of being dissected by white interviewers on how ethnic I was. Am I active enough? Do I hang with "my people"? Do I fight for students? On one hand I am supposed to fit the stereotype of the activist, able to bond with those needy Hispanic students; but they don't want that type of colleague because they are aggressive and not interested in real scholarship. I felt that being an authentic minority and a good candidate are diametrically opposed. So what can we do as women of color to make real gains within this system?

.   .   .

We ourselves must learn not to try to find our power in an institution that constantly threatens to destroy us; and I believe we must teach young women of color this as well. We must not become insulated in our small successes but always remember Barbara Smith's statement that "Surviving as a Black woman has been a victory, with sanity intact, you know?" (Lorde 1992 in Gomez 1996, 202). We indeed must become like Audre Lorde's Sister Outsider so "'divide and conquer' [can] become 'define and power'" (Lorde 1992 in Gomez 1996, 112). In whatever role we serve in the academy, we must prepare other women of color for life in Lorde's symphony: as junior faculty we can enliven and challenge our senior colleagues' ideas and approaches; as senior faculty we can actively support our colleagues and students and challenge administrative policies and procedure; as chairs of departments we can look for ways to help graduate and undergraduate students throughout the system and foster curricula change; as teachers we can promote the need to think and act critically in the world; we can discuss the construction and power of institutions; as students of color we can train ourselves to fight the system; as women of color we need to support each other and continue to survive, in spite of the system, keeping hope that we might be able to join to conceive of anew system that would include many visions. We must remember our anger towards the injustice of the present system and translate that anger into power.

If I have realized one thing through this agonizing process of searching for a job as an academic, it is that one person can change the institution—she can create space for change on all levels. If we want to be more than ghosts in the academic machine, or token without influence, we must constantly be willing to challenge the sites of power that exist and also to deny the ancient meanings of the positions we might hold or strive to hold. We must instead re-envision those positions so that they can support and foster us, as well as those who will follow us.

* * *

Assistant Professor of English Gil-Gomez did find success on the job market. After her second year of interviewing, after having a much clearer sense of academic power structures, she accepted a position in a small department. She is the only person of color in her program. Her hope is that her colleagues "don't really believe they have found their academic Elvis." Her fingers are crossed that her position is a good match.

5. Encourage Faculty Candidates to Ask Questions of the Search Committee.

Assistant Professor of Economics Ranjeeta Ghiara invites faculty candidates to ask questions of their interviewers and for the search committees to encourage candidates to ask questions. She told us, "It is not fair to expect answers magically. We need to allow applicants to ask questions about our questions. This will help them to contextualize the questions." We might add, allowing faculty candidates to ask questions of the search committee helps candidates demonstrate their knowledge.

6. Be Aware of the Awkward Situations you Create for Candidates.

- *Have you designed tricky teaching presentations?* Several contributors commented that at their campus interviews, they were asked to teach someone else's class. As we discussed in chapter 4, your search committee may elect to create an extemporaneous teaching presentation by giving the candidate ten minutes to prepare a class on a particular topic. If your colleagues intend to include this presentation in candidates' interviews, ask the committee what the interview value of such a rushed class preparation is. Surely your program does not advocate professors spending only ten minutes in preparation for class.

- *How do you offer the job to your department's "second choice" candidate?* Director of the Center for Teaching and Learning at California State University, Sacramento, Alan Kalish told us the story of one of the new faculty hires he interviewed for his dissertation project. The faculty candidate who was told she was the committee's second choice after the first choice candidate from a prestigious school withdrew his application. What a kind way to welcome a potentially new colleague!

7. Recognize How Your Committee Evaluates Noncredential Issues.

- *Are evaluations based on faculty candidates' perceived age?* Youthful appearances apparently don't benefit faculty candidates. Several contributors commented that looking young made search committees question their ability to be taken seriously, especially if they were being hired for administrative positions. Others found that they had to take extra care to clarify their training and teaching experience; their in-coming salaries depended on this clarification. When they didn't point out their experience, some candidates with eight to ten years of teaching experience were "read" as new Ph.D's with no experience. In other words, their *vitae* were skimmed over because, of course, the candidates looked too young to have experience. Don't be too sure that you know how old your candidates are or that knowing their age really matters.

- *Is regional prejudice evident?* Several contributors told us that search committees actually told them that transplants from certain states or parts of the country would not be welcome in the community. Other candidates were told that they didn't fit the stereotype of people from the Southwest, Midwest, South, or Southern California.

8. Be Scrupulous About the Reasons You Reject Candidates.

Be careful how you phrase the bad news. The way in which you reject candidates may force faculty candidates to feel that they don't belong to the profession at all. While generic letters are distant, they are more respectful than telling candidates that the new hire "simply has the most impressive credentials." Also be certain to address these letters properly. Some contributors commented that they received rejections for positions for which they didn't apply.

9. Train Faculty to Interview

As Assistant Professor of Psychology Gina Grimshaw reminds us, "Faculty members are not great interviewers. There is no training in it." We would all certainly benefit from interview training. You may want to call on your university's human resources management office for assistance in this area.

10. Consciously Prepare Graduate Students to Teach.

Most graduate students will not find jobs at top-notch research institutes where research may be emphasized over teaching. Instead, most graduate students will secure jobs that value teaching and research equally or that valorize teaching. Alan Kalish, Director of the Center for Teaching and Learning at California State University, Sacramento, argues in his forthcoming dissertation, "[T]he profession would benefit if legitimate, nonexploitative post-doctoral positions were created to enable some new Ph.D.'s to develop their teaching capital and understanding of local culture and institutions other than their graduate school." And Acting Instructor Mark Long explains, "[M]ost graduate students build professional narratives that are incommensurate with the professional lives they will likely lead." While you want to set challenging goals for your graduate students, always be certain to link your students' skills in ways that will benefit them on the job market.

Success on the job market doesn't need to be mystery. Thoughtful graduate curricula that include forums on the state of the profession and workshops and one-on-one assistance on preparing for academic job searches will only strengthen higher education. Cheers to honest preparation for and success on the real academic job market!

Finding a Job Announcement in Your Field

The list of publications and webistes that follows is not intended to be a complete list for all academic fields. The list should, however, help you recognize the range of sources you may wish to consult as you begin your job search. Most of the job list sources include both academic and non-academic job opportunities. The best way to locate academic and non-academic jobs is to consult as many sources as possible: websites, mentors, employed friends, colleagues, scholarly journals and job lists, and the material a hiring institution itself puts out. Here are some sources to get you started.

Anthropology

Degree	*Job List Source*
M.A. or Ph.D.	"American Anthropological Association" newsletter is best place to access academic positions for anthropologists.

Art

Degree	*Job List Source*
M.A., M.F.A., or Ph.D.	On-line source: *http://www.collegeart.org* CAA Careers, a comprehensive listing of employment oppurtunities for artists, art historians, and

other visual arts professionals is published bi-monthly (in October, December, February, April, June, and August). To subscribe, e-mail CAA Member Services at membership@collegeart.org. Include your name and street address and a membership/subscription application will be mailed to you (electronic applications are not available at this time.)

Biological Sciences

Degree	*Job List Source*
M.A. or Ph.D.	*Science* and *Nature* (available in hardcopy and on-line).

Business (Management)

Degree

B.A., M.A., or Ph.D.

Job List Source

1) On-line Sources:
   a) http:/Classified2000.com
   b) http:/employment.classified.yahoo.com
2) Management Positions: "Placement Roster" published twice a year by the Academy of Management which lists available positions as well as candidates who are on the market.
3) Management Positions On-line Source—Academy of Management Homepage: http://www.aom.pace.edu
Note: Marketing and Accounting candidates need to locate similar sources produced by their fields' national organizations.

Chemistry

Degree

M.A. or Ph.D.

Job List Source

1) *Chemical & Engineering News*
2) *Chronicle of Higher Education*
3) On-line Source: http://chronicle.com

Communication Studies

Degree

M.A. or Ph.D.

Job List Source

1) *Spectra* from the National Communication Association, 5105 Backlick Road, Bldg. E, Annandale, VA 22003.

2) On-line Source: Send an email message to Comserve@cios.llc.rpi.edu Type "Show Hotlines" in body of text.

Composition and Rhetoric

Degree   *Job List Source*
M.A. or Ph.D.   1) *MLA Job List*
                           2) *Chronicle of Higher Education*
                           3) On-line Source: http://chronicle.com

Dance

Degree   *Job List Source*
M.A., M.F.A., or Ph.D.   Publications of the College Art Association, New York

Economics

Degree   *Job List Source*
M.A. or Ph.D.   1) *Job Openings for Economists* (JOE) available by writing or calling Job Openings for Economists, 2014 Broadway, Suite 305, Nashville, TN 37203. The fax number is 615-343-7590.
                           2) *Chronicle of Higher Education*
                           3) On-line Sources:
                               a) http://chronicle.com
                               b) http://www.eco.utexas.edu/joe/

Education

Degree   *Job List Source*
M.A., ED. D., or Ph.D.   1) *American Educational Research Association* (AERA)
                           2) *Association for Educational Communications and Technology* (AECT); both journals publish job openings, send job announcements to colleges to post for their graduates, and provide job interviews at their annual conferences.
                           3) On-line Sources:
                               a)http://204.252.76.75:80/ Employment/Employment.htm
                               b) http://www.columbia.edu/~sss31/ Education/jobs.html

Foreign Languages

Degree	*Job List Source*
M.A. or Ph.D.	1) *MLA Job List,* Foreign Language Edition
	2) *Chronicle of Higher Education*
	3) Almost every language has its own national organization that publishes a journal, such as the American Association of Teachers of Spanish and Portuguese, which publishes *Hispania.*
	4) On-line sources:
	a) The Agora Language Marketplace: http://agoralang.com/agora/prof.html
	b) International Language Jobs: http://www.europa-pages.co.uk/job_form.html

Geography

Degree	*Job List Source*
M.A. or Ph.D.	1) "The Association of American Geographers(AAG) Newsletter."
	2) On-line Source: http://www.aag.org

History

Degree	*Job List Source*
M.A. or Ph.D.	1) *Chronicle of Higher Education*
	2) *Perspectives* (a publication of the American Historical Association).
	3) On-line Source: H-Net's Job Guide for the Humanities and Social Sciences: http://www.matrix.msu.edu/jobs/

Humanities

Degree	*Job List Source*
M.A. or Ph.D.	1) *Chronicle of Higher Education*
	2) On-line Sources:
	a) http://chronicle.com
	b) H-Net's Job Guide for the Humanities and

Social Sciences:
http://www.matrix.msu.edu/jobs/

Latin American Studies

Degree	*Job List Source*
M.A or Ph.D.	On-line Sources: The Latin American Studies Association's (LASA) Electronic Employment Bulletin Board: http://www.pitt.edu/~lasa/employment.htm

Literature

Degree
M.A. or Ph.D.

Job List Source
1) *MLA Job List*
2) *Chronicle of Higher Education*
3) On-line Source: http://chronicle.com

Linguistics

Degree
M.A. or Ph.D.

Job List Source
1) *American Psychological Association (APA) Monitor*
2) *American Psychological Society (APS) Observer*
3) *Chronicle of Higher Education*
4) On line Sources:
    a) http://chronicle.com
    b) *Linguistic Society of America (LSA) Bulletin*: http://www.lsa.org

Mathematics

Degree
M.A. or Ph.D.

Job List Source
1) *FOCUS*, The newsletter of the Mathematical Association of America.
2) *Notices of the American Mathematical Society*
3) *Chronicle of Higher Education*
4) On-line Sources:
    a) http://chronicle.com
    b) http://e-math.ams.org/ (See "Employment in Mathematical Science Listings")

Music

Degree	*Job List Source*
M.A. or Ph.D.	The College Music Society Newsletter (bi-monthly)
	202 W. Spruce Street
	Missoula, MT 29802-4202
	406-721-9619
	406-721-9419 fax
	cms@music.org e-mail

Philosophy

Degree

Job List Source

1) *Jobs for Philosophers Quarterly*, published by the American Philosophical Association.

2) *Chronicle of Higher Education*

3) On-line Sources:
  a) http://www.matrix.msu.edu/jobs/
  b) http://www.udel.edu/apa/

Physics

Degree

M.A. or Ph.D.

Job List Source

1) *Physics Today*

2) *Chronicle of Higher Education*

3) On-line Source: http://chronicle.com

Political Science

Degree

M.A. or Ph.D.

Job List Source

1) American Political Science Association's "Personnel Service Newsletter."

2) *Chronicle of Higher Education*

3) On-line Source: H-Net's Job Guide for the Humanities and Social Sciences: http://www.matrix.msu.edu/jobs/

Psychology

Degree

M.A. or Ph.D.

Job List Source

1) *Chronicle of Higher Education*, the primary source for academic postions, especially for those in experimental psychology.

2) *Monitor*, a publication of the American

Psychological Association (APA). This is a useful resource for locating clinical positions, post-docs, and internships.

3) *Observer*, a publication of the American Psychological Society (APS).

4) For community college positions, contact the individual campuses.

Sociology

Degree	*Job List Source*
M.A. or Ph.D.	ACADEMIC POSITIONS

1) American Sociological Association's (ASA) *Employment Bulletin*. Available in hard copy by subscription or listed monthly on-line. Note: the on-line version is not archived.

2) *Chronicle of Higher Education*

3) On-line Sources.

    a) http://chronicle.com

    b) http//www.chronicle.com/jobs/

    c) http://www.asanet.org

APPLIED POSITIONS

1) On-line Sources:

    a) http//:www.asanet.org; American Sociological Association's (ASA) *Employment Bulletin*. Check the links to other corporate, applied, and government jobs sites.

    b) http:// www.epn.org; the Electronic Policy Network list provides over thirty organizations and has a job board. There are also many consulting firms, both non-profit and for-profit.

    c) The Society for Applied Sociology: http://www.appliedsoc.org;

    d)   The Sociological Practice Association : http://www.erols.com/jandjb/SPAhome.htm

    e)   The Professional Association in Sociology: http://www.jcu.edu/SOCIO/assoc.htm. This web site has links to the various professional associations, including regional associations which also list both academic and applied jobs. 2) Federal and state governments hire a large number of sociologists annually. The place to look on the federal level is the job listings for each agency, e.g. NIH (National Institutes of Health); NIDA (Drug and Alcohol); NICHD (Child Health and Development); NIA (Aging); NIJ (Justice); etc. Also look at places like Commerce and Transportation and the Center for Disease Control. 3) On the state level, people should look at state agencies, Social Services, Commerce, Health, Transportation, and Justice.

Theater

Degree   *Job List Source*

M.A., M.F.A, or Ph.D.   Publications of the Theater Communications Group, New York.

Women's Studies

Degree   *Job List Source*

M.A. or Ph.D.   1) *National Women's Studies Association* (NWSA) journal
2) *Chronicle of Higher Education*
3) *MLA Job List*
4) On-line Source: http://chronicle.com

Getting Help in Developing Your Professional Life

You may also appreciate insight from websites designed specifically for future faculty.
Dr. Janice A. Smith, the director of the Preparing Future Faculty program at the University of Minnesota, suggests the following:
www.aacu-edu.org
www.egshet.org
www.p-faculty.org

Electronic Job Banks and Job Search Resources

Because of the interactive nature of job searches over the Web, applicants should also look at general job banks. Many of these sites allow applicants to post resumes, and most, if not all, also allow keyword searches by job type, region, and salary. Some also have international sites, especially pertinent for foreign languages and research.

Assistant Professor of Business Jerome Curry has collected the following electronic information for his business writing students. He cautions: "Keep in mind, however, that Internet sites have a limited shelf life." If one of these sites has disappeared by the time you try to access it, try the others. One site can lead you to many other links.

Netscape Navigator Guide: The Online Handbook

http://home.netscape.com/eng/mozilla/2.0/handbook/
For help using Netscape Navigator consult this online handbook. It provides an easy-to-understand tutorial as well as a detailed explanation of Netscape's features.

Internet Job Search Guides

A good way to begin your job search is by consulting some Internet job search guides. In addition to supplying access to job openings, job search guides provide—or provide links to—a great deal of additional helpful information, such as tips for preparing an effective cover letter and resume, hints that may help you during the interview, relocation resources, hiring trends, starting salaries, etc. Seven of the best are listed below.

America's Employers: The Job Seeker's Home on the Internet

http://americasemployers.com
This is, at present, arguably the best of the job search guides, offering a comprehensive and easy-to-use set of tools for the job seeker. Its Career Chat floor is a real plus. It makes it possible for candidates to converse with potential employers and to network with professionals in their field—in real time.

CareerMosaic

http://www.careermosaic.com/cm/home.html
Career Mosaic is one of the few employment-related sites that devotes a section—College Connection—to internships and entry-level job opportunities.

E-Span

http://www.espan.com/
E-Span's database of jobs is extensive and is updated twice weekly—Monday and Wednesday. A good many of the opportunities offered, however, are for engineers, accountants, and computer scientists.

Job Web

http://www.jobweb.org/
Among its many resources Job Web also offers links to a variety of online career sites for the differently abled: http://www.jobweb.org/catapult/disabled/htm

The Monster Board

http://www.monster.com
The Monster Board offers one of the largest online job databases. It claims

to have over 55,000 job opportunities available. More than 15,000 are from its own database and 40,000 from job-related newsgroups. The Board adds 1500 news jobs per week to its list.

The Riley Guide

http://www.dbm.com/jobguide
This site provides a wealth of valuable job search information. Especially helpful is its guide to the online job search (Click on "I'd like some help with this"). Additionally, The Riley Guide supplies links to an impressive selection of online job lists.

Virtual Job Fair

http://www.careerexpo.com/
Virtual Job Fair is affiliated with the magazine *High Technology Careers*. Not surprisingly, then, a good many of the more than 15,000 jobs listed are for engineers and computer scientists.

Cover Letter Writing Guide: Cover Letters

http://www.rpi.edu/dept/llc/writecenter/web/text/coverltr.html
For a brief but informative introduction to writing the cover letter, consult this site. Two effective sample letters are offered as models.

Resume Writing Guides: How to Write an Exceptional Resume

http://www.his.com/~rockport/resumes.htm
This guide focuses on the traditional (as opposed to the electronic) resume. It will take you step-by-step through the resume-writing process and promises that the outcome will be "powerful and effective." The advice offered, however, while clear, thorough, and helpful, is in many ways intended for job searchers with experience in their field. Nonetheless, individuals seeking an entry-level position should not ignore this guide. Despite its bias toward the experienced job searcher, there is much that they can learn from it.

How to Write an Electronic Resume

http:/222.occ.com/occ/JLK/HowToEResume.html
This document provides the novice e-resume writer with a list of tips.

General Job Listings Sites

These sites offer access to jobs in a wide variety of professions. Some also provide modest job search guidance.

CareerPath

http://www.careerpath.com/index.html
Career Path will allow you to browse over 200,000 employment ads from forty-one major newspapers throughout the United States.

HeadHunter.NET

http://www.HeadHunter.NET/
HeadHunter.NET can be valuable to those jobseekers who are looking for a certain type of job in a specific location and who have a specific salary in mind. This site allows you to focus your search on any city you desire both inside and outside the continental United States.

HEART/Career Connections

http://www.career.com/PUB/heart.html
Be certain to check this site's calendar for upcoming HEART-sponsored job fairs. These so-called CyberFairs™ allow participants to meet with potential employers and to converse with them privately online and in real-time. And, best of all, this service is free.

IntelliMatch

http://www.intellimatch.com/
This site includes a time-saving feature called Job Agent. All you need to do is to enter your employment preferences, and Job Agent will automatically and continuously search the site's database for matching jobs. Job Agent— not the jobseeker—performs this annoying and tedious task. When a match is found, you will be promptly notified by e-mail.

The Internet Job Locator

http://www.joblocator.com/jobs/
This site allows you to post your resume to as many as ten Usenet (a network of electronic bulletin boards) newsgroups instantly. Just fill out the on-screen form and save it to their database. Then choose the newsgroups

to which you would like your resume posted and click on *Post News*. It's that simple.

OnlineCareerCenter

http://www.occ.com
If you post your resume to only one site, make this it. OCC claims to have access to over 30 million online subscribers.

Profession-Specific Job Listings Sites:

As the heading suggests, these sites focus on specific professions. Do not, however, restrict your search to one of these sites simply because it focuses on your field of interest. The job lists indicated above, though general in nature, may offer additional employment opportunities and should not be overlooked.

The Business Job Finder

http://www.cob.ohio state.edu/dept/fin/osujobs.htm

The Chronicle of Higher Education

http://chronicle.com
The *Chronicle* website is a superb resource. Job announcements are available free via the web one week after they're made available to paying *Chronicle* subscribers. While default links organize information by discipline or by type of job, the *Chronicle* job link is also searchable by keyword and by geographical region. Announcements listed include faculty, executive, administrative, and non-academic jobs openings, with each category linked to several subcategories. Many of the institutions advertising openings have also provided a hot link to their home pages. Additional links include a bibliography of search-related publications, interviews with academic and non-academic search committees, and current news about the state of the academy.

Journalism Jobs

http://ng120-3.journalism.berkeley,edu/resources/jobs/

MedSearchAmerica(healthcare)

http://www.medsearch.com

Interview Guide: Job Interview Tips

http://www.claitors.com/ooh/ooh00012.htm

Preparing Future Faculty

http://www.umn.edu/ohr/pff
This site provides useful information for those graduate students who are considering employment in higher education. The site is also useful for those institutions interested in designing programs to prepare future faculty.

Usenet Access Site

The following launchpad makes accessing Usenet's network of electronic bulletins board a relatively simple task.

Usenet Information Center Launchpad

http://sunsite.unc.edu/usenet-b/home.html

Some Popular Search Engines for the Web and Usenet

AltaVista

http:www.altavista.digital.com/

DejaNews

http://www.dejanews.com/

exciteNetsearch

http://excite.com/

HotBot

http://www.hotbot.com/

Lycos

http://fuzine.mt.cs.cmu.edu/mlm/lycos-home.html

Yahoo!

http://www/yahoo.com/

For more field specific academic job search information, see Appendix 1.

APPENDIX III

Job Search Workshop

Casie Hermansson and Margaret McGeachy put together this marvelous job workshop with fellow graduate students when they found themselves without funding to attend the discipline's conference workshop. The two-part workshop they designed represents a savvy proactive response to the academic job search. Hermansson described the success of the workshop:

> Quite apart from the good advice and peer-editing I received through the seminar and workshop, I also received unsolicited letters of recommendation for service in my file. It was eight weeks after this workshop, and four months before I defended, when my practice runs actually produced an unexpected response. I had telephone and campus interviews, and a job offer which I accepted. While there is no traceable correlation, the dean did raise the topic of this seminar during my interview with him, and it clearly made a favorable impression in terms of service.

Below is the workshop description Hermansson forwarded to us. We thank her and McGeachy for giving us permission to include the workshop here.

Designing Your English Academic Dossier

PART I

The workshop started on a Friday in early April, as classes were ending. We began the day with coffee and muffins (sponsored by the graduate association). Our first speaker was our placement officer, on "The *vita* and its Adjuncts" (related documents like the research statement). After a mid-morning break, we had a second guest speaker on "The Teaching Dossier"— what it is, and what information to be collecting as graduate assistants to make some case for teaching experience. We were able to take all of the guest speakers (eight in all) to lunch with funds obtained from the department. The afternoon began with a representative from the Graduate Dossier Service. The remainder was a roundtable moderated by a fellow student featuring three senior faculty with hiring committee experience and two recent hires with job search experience. As expected, there was little consensus, dramatizing an important lesson about attempting to second-guess a hiring committee or to privilege any one "way" of approaching the job market.

The university bookstore agreed to sponsor our event by making professional flyers advertising the event. They had a table at the event featuring relevant titles we had asked them to order. The Modern Language Association (MLA) sent several free copies of a related issue of *Profession* which we were able to use. Also available for sale at cost were custom-published readers we had tailor-made the way a course reader is produced. These were done through the bookstore, subject to copyright restrictions, and presented articles on all aspects of the job search which we compiled from difficult to find sources. The *ADE Bulletin*, for instance, has any number of helpful articles, and even special issues, devoted to the topic, but this was not available in our library and was obtained instead from private subscribers. As the custom-published template is now on file, it is available for order by future students. Finally, we had a bulky handout (reproduced through the placement office for us) of various sample documents, as well as an open letter from our teaching coordinator, another from a recently hired graduate on her search process, a couple of rejection letters, and the university contract letter for good measure.

PART II

Those wishing to participate in the follow-up workshop could use the samples, choosing a job announcement from those we included to frame their practice "application," as they were asked to bring drafts of their documents to the relevant workshop day (see list below).

We asked all of our speakers to have a very practical focus and to talk mostly about the documents. We hoped to discover methods by which to feel more competent in the one area over which the candidate does have control—self-presentation in the application package. The day therefore worked well as an informative precursor to a five-part workshop which followed the presentation by a week. The workshop involved a much smaller group of interested students, many of whom had taken advantage of the event to open a file, order transcripts, and consider their list of referees as a first step. It was facilitated by both the outgoing and incoming placement officers, and featured two guest students "fresh" from their campus interviews. We had booked a room for two hours each morning for a week. The schedule was the following:

Monday:	*vita*
Tuesday:	Statement of Teaching Philosophy
Wednesday:	Dissertation Abstract/Research Statement
Thursday:	Reading and Researching Jobs
Friday:	Application Letter and Completed Dossier

The workshop involved putting some of our attempts on overhead projectors and discussing. Each day the discussions continued after the workshops. The workshop sequence fostered the exchange of ideas with peers and with the placement officers.

Sample Cover Letters and Vitae

Sample Business Management *Vita* for a Tenure-Track Position at a Research/Teaching University

---

BEVERLY J. MORALES

Home Address   Office Address

10635 SW 74th Terrace   Department of Management
Miami, FL 33173   East Coast University
(305) 274-1569   414 Smith Building
                                Virginia Beach, VA 23452
                                (757) 284-5846

Education

| East Coast University | 6/87–present | Ph.D. (expected 5/91) in Business Administration (Concentration in Organizational Behavior) |
| East Coast University | 8/84–5/87 | B.A. in Psychology |

Academic Awards and Honors

Included in *Who's Who Among Students in American Universities and Colleges, 1990.*

Nominated to attend the Doctoral Student Consortium, Organizational Behavior and Organization Theory Divisions, 50th Annual Meeting of the Academy of Management, San Francisco, California, 1990.

Graduated with Honors from East Coast University.

Undergraduate Dean's List and President's Honor Roll each semester while attending East Coast University.

Memberships and Honor Societies

Student affiliate of the Academy of Management since Fall 1989.

Student affiliate of the Southern Management Association since Fall 1989.

Lifetime member of Phi Kappa Phi National Honor Society.

Lifetime member of Golden Key National Honor Society.

Academic Employment Experience

Teaching Assistant	Spring 1990– Present	Management Department
Research Assistant	Fall 1987– Spring 1990	Management Department
Teaching Assistant for Leadership and Motivation (graduate)	Intersession 1990 and Summer 1990	Management Department
Adjunct Instructor for Organizational Behavior (undergraduate)	Fall 1990 and Spring 1991	Management Department
Adjunct Instructor for Industrial Psychology (undergraduate)	Fall 1990 and Spring 1991	Psychology Department

Publications and Manuscripts Under Review

Smith, C. A., Morales, B.J., & Hilt, K. D. The effect of negation and polar opposite item reversals on questionnaire reliability and validity: An experimental investigation. "Educational and Psychological Measurement," in press.

Smith, C. A., & Morales, B. J. (1989). Item wording effects on factor analytic results: An experimental investigation using LISREL confirmatory analysis. "Journal of Applied Psychology," under second review.

Smith, C. A., & Morales, B. J. Item wording effects on exploratory factor-analytic results: An experimental investigation. "Proceedings of the Annual Meeting of the Southern Management Association," Atlanta, 1989.

Smith, C. A., & Morales, B. J. A LISREL confirmatory factor-analytic investigation of item wording effects on the obtained factor structures of survey questionnaire data. Accepted for publication in the "Proceedings of the Annual Meeting of the Southern Management Association," Baton Rouge, 1990.

Dissertation Research in Progress

Mentoring and charismatic leadership as related processes in organizational behavior (Doctoral Dissertation, supervised by C. A. Smith, expected completion date 5/91).

References

Dr. Chester A. Smith
Department of Management
East Coast University
414 Smith Building
Virginia Beach, VA
(757) 284-5846

Dr. John W. Baker
Department of Management
East Coast University
414 Smith Building
Virginia Beach, VA
(757) 284-5846

Dr. Linda L. Neil
Department of Management
East Coast University

Dr. Donald K. Rent
Department of Psychology
East Coast University

414 Smith Building   208 Jefferson Building
Virginia Beach, VA   Virginia Beach, VA
(757) 284-5846   (305) 284-2814

Sample Humanities Cover Letter for a Tenure-Track Position at a Research/Teaching University

November 5, 1994

Chair
Literature Studies Search Committee
CSU Dominguez Hills, California 90196

Dear Search Committee,

I am writing in response to your search for a specialist in Composition and Rhetoric at the rank of Assistant Professor, advertised in the October *MLA Job Information List*. I am presently a Ph.D. candidate in the Rhetoric, Linguistics, and Literature program in the English department at West Coast University. I will complete the requirements for my degree by May 1995.

My dissertation, entitled "Changing an Embodied Writing Ideology: A Womanist Critique" is a feminist-historical study of composition theory and pedagogy. In it I explore how Romantic ideology, physical space, and collaborative theories influence contemporary feminist composition scholarship. Chapters 1 and 2 establish how Romanticism has shaped our profession and its institutions and suggest that this framework, renowned for celebrating the male self, contributes to the effacement of female subjectivity. Chapter 3 argues that this gender distinction relies upon a sexist evaluation of "genius," and that this splitting of the imagination into the primary and the secondary results in what might be termed Romantic language theory. Chapter 4 connects seemingly disparate paradigmatic shifts, namely that of language and that of family, by considering Charlotte Perkins Gilman's "The Yellow Wallpaper" and Virginia Woolf's *A Room of One's Own*. Their works suggest how Romantic language theory entangles women. Then in a chapter written in collaboration with Anne Welsh, I consider the ways collaborative theory, a significant pedagogical and theoretical response to the gender-privileging of Romanticism, is challenged by the patriarchal and familial language it employs. My study concludes by arguing that some contemporary feminist reclamations of the imagination and "genius" dismantle the collective response to Romanticism because of their inward-turning theories and pedagogies.

My scholarship contributes to current conversations in composition and rhetoric. The theoretical framework of my dissertation is similar to the one that informs *The Romantic Legacy*, a book I am co-editing, which is currently being reviewed by Heinemann-Boynton/Cook. Also Chapter 5 of my dissertation is being reviewed for inclusion in the *First National Writing Centers Association Conference Anthology*, a book whose general editors include Eric James, Christina Jones, and Byron Stacey.

My research interests include composition and feminist theories. I am especially intrigued by the ways in which these theories and British and American texts of the nineteenth and twentieth centuries prove to be mutually illuminating.

These research interests allow me to make connections among composition and literary research and practice. My extensive experience in composition classrooms and in writing centers, teaching multi-cultural populations, and my participation in developing curriculum and policy as a Coordinator in West Coast University's Freshman Writing Program encourage me to join theory and pedagogy. Furthermore, my role as a Coordinator in West Coast University's large, innovative writing program provides me with considerable experience implementing yearly orientations and training programs for new and returning instructors which are grounded in current theories and practice. Finally, I appreciate the opportunity to bring literature and composition studies together in the upper-division humanities/literature course I teach at California State College. Each of these teaching and administrative roles continues to challenge me to find better ways to bridge theory and practice.

Finally, as the Managing Editor of *The Writing Teacher*, a nationally distributed journal addressing current issues in composition and rhetoric, I have experience addressing many of the administrative and theoretical issues that pertain to publishing. As the editor, I oversee all aspects of publication, including manuscript submissions and review.

I enclose my *vita* and dissertation abstract. Confidential credentials are on file with the Graduate Placement Service at West Coast University. To request my dossier, please contact me. I will request that the placement service forward it to you.

I would be pleased to discuss my qualifications further with you at the upcoming MLA Convention in San Diego. Until December 18, I can be contacted at West Coast University or at my home: 976 Flores St. #231, West Hollywood, CA 90069, Phone: (310) 652-0689. After December 18 and until January 3, I can be reached at (619) 759-9815. I look forward to hearing from you.

Thank you for your consideration.

Sincerely,
Ann M. Hein

Sample Humanities Vita for a Tenure-Track Position at a Research/Teaching University

---

Ann M. Hein
976 Flores Street
West Hollywood, California 90069
(310) 652-0689

EDUCATION:

Ph.D.(1995) English (Rhetoric, Linguistics, and Literature)
West Coast University

M.A. (1992) English
West Coast University

Graduate Work (1990–1991) American/English Literature
Southern California State, San Diego

B.A. (1990) *summa cum laude*
Majors: English Literature and Communication Studies
San Diego University

DISSERTATION:

"Changing an Embodied Writing Ideology: A Womanist Critique"

Committee: James A. Ross (Chair)
              Michael Greene
              Susan Richlin

ACADEMIC HONORS:

(1994–1995) Managing Editor of *The Writing Teacher*
(1994–1995) Freshman Writing Program "Outstanding Teaching
  Assistant Award"
(1990) Kappa Gamma Pi Honor Society
(1990) English Department, "Highest Department Honors"
(1990) Communication Studies, "Highest Department Honors"
(1990) Writing Center, "Writing Center Award"
(1986–1990) University of San Diego Academic Scholarship

TEACHING INTERESTS:

Theory and History of Rhetoric and Composition
Composition (including courses for non-native speakers)
British and American Romanticism
Feminist Theory and Criticism

PUBLICATIONS:

"Tickling the Student's Ear: Collaboration and the Teacher/Student
  Relationship." Chapter in the *First National Writing Centers Association
  Conference Anthology*. General Editors: Eric James, Christina Jones, and
  Byron Stacey
"The Erotics of the Pen in the Teacher/Student Relationship." Journal arti-
  cle being revised for publication.
"Womanist-Feminist Composition: A Placebo Power with Potential."
  Journal article being revised for publication.
Feminist Composition Theory and Practice: An Anthology. Book edited by Ann M. Hein
  and Anne Welsh. The book arranges feminist composition and rhetorical
  scholarship according to metaphors that mark the field. In progress.
"Samuel Taylor Coleridge." Entry on Samuel Taylor Coleridge forthcoming in
  Encyclopedia of Rhetoric and Linguistsics. Silver Publishing. Editor: Terry Esther.

"Becoming Literate in the Employment Line: Graduate Students' Strategies for Job Placement." ERIC 1995.

"The Politics of Space in (Feminist) Composition Theory." *ERIC* 1994.

Managing Editor, *The Writing Teacher* 14.3 (1995). (Issue Theme: "Writing the Self into the Social.")

Managing Editor, *The Writing Teacher* 14.2 (1995). (Issue Theme: "Searching for Literacy.")

Managing Editor, *The Writing Teacher* 14.1 (1994). (Issue Theme: "Positioning Composition in the Academy.")

Editor, *The Writing Teacher* 13.3 (1994). (Issue Theme: "Popular Culture in the Composition Classroom.")

"Popular Culture in the Composition Classroom." (With R. Kevin Taylor). *The Writing Teacher* 13:3 (1994): 99–100.

Editor, *The Writing Teacher* 12:2 (1993). (Issue Theme: "Bridging the Ethical Gap: Pedagogy and Theory in the Classroom.")

"Bridging the Ethical Gap: Pedagogy and Theory in the Classroom." *The Writing Teacher* 12:2 (1993): 51–52.

ACADEMIC POSITIONS:

West Coast University

1991–1995   *Freshman Writing Program*
Assistant Lecturer; designing and teaching sequenced freshman writing courses which develop the students' use of rhetorical skills as they pertain to critical thinking, reading, and writing.

1991–1993   *Writing Center*
Consultant; working with undergraduate and graduate students on their critical analysis and writing skills.

California State College, Los Angeles

1994   *Program for Adult College Education*
Humanities Instructor; designing and teaching an upper-division humanities/literature class the focus of which is a critique of success and values in the U.S.

Malibu City College

1993–1995   *Writing and Reading Center*
                         Writing Instructor; designing and implementing
                         individual composition curricula for undergradu-
                         ate students, focusing largely on the writing needs
                         of non-native speakers of English.

Southern California State, San Diego

1991   *College Writing Program*
                         Teaching Assistant; designing and teaching an
                         advanced, freshman writing course which gives stu-
                         dents the ability to analyze the rhetorical devices
                         writers employ and to develop the students'
                         rhetorical skills as they pertain to their own writing.

San Diego University

1988–1990   *Writing Center*
                         Writing Center Peer Tutor; tutoring peers in
                         their critical analysis and writing skills.

ACADEMIC AND ADMINISTRATIVE SERVICE:

West Coast University

1994–1995   *The Writing Teacher*
                         Managing Editor; organizing and overseeing all
                         aspects of publication for this nationally distrib-
                         uted journal, including manuscript submissions
                         and review, publicity, and budget management.

1993–1994   Assistant Managing Editor

1991–1993   Editorial Board Member

1993–Present   *Freshman Writing Program (FWP)*
                         Instructional Coordinator; assisting in planning and
                         conducting instructor orientation and first-year
                         instructor training; improving and implementing
                         FWP curriculum; developing proposals on
                         curricular and pedagogical issues to be considered
                         by the FWP Policy Committee; planning and
                         conducting the staff development program for

continuing instructors; serving as a group leader for midterm diagnostic and final portfolio readings; working to improve communication between FWP administration and instructors.

1994–1995   *FWP Policy Committee*
Assistant Lecturer Representative; presenting ALs' perspectives as they pertain to specific program policies and to the committee's recommended redesign of the writing program.

1994   *FWP Textbook Committee*
Member; selecting a range of readers, rhetorics, and handbooks appropriate for the sequence of composition courses FWP offers and preparing an annotated bibliography of our selections.

1994   *West Coast University*
Spring Rhetoric Conference
Academic Conference Co-chair; organizing and implementing the conference; (Speakers: Jay Cohen and Susan McLeod.)

Blox Press
1994   Manuscript Reviewer; providing criticism for a second edition of Charles Brown and Charlie Van Snoy's reader, *Readings in Culture, Identity, and Values.*

San Diego University
1989–1990   *Writing Center*
Student-Coordinator; organizing and supervising a 60-tutor program in order to satisfy the needs of approximately 1100 students each semester; planning and implementing weekly tutor training seminars.

1990   Research Assistant; editing Dr. Linda A.M. Perry's co-authored book, *Constructing and Reconstructing Gender: The Links Among Communication, Language, and Gender* (New York: State U of New York P, 1992).

ACADEMIC PRESENTATIONS AND WORKSHOPS:

"Becoming Literate in the Employment Line: Graduate Students' Strategies
for Job Placement." *Conference on College Composition and
Communication.* Washington, D.C. 23 March 1995.

"Re-invigorating the Comp 101/102 Curricula." (With Anne Welsh and Jim
Adams). The Fall 1994 Freshman Writing Program Staff Development
Presentation and Workshop. Los Angeles. 30 August 1994.

"Re-imag(in)ing the Writing Instructor (a.k.a. Tutor)." (With Carolyn Heinz,
Renee Buchovich, and Anne Welsh). *The National Writing Centers
Association Conference.* New Orleans, Louisiana. 14 April 1994.

"Tickling the Student's Ear: Collaboration and the Teacher/Student
Relationship." (With Anne Welsh). *The National Graduate Women's
Studies Conference.* UC, San Diego, California. 15 April 1994.

"The Politics of Space in (Feminist) Composition Theory." *Conference on
College Composition and Communication.* Nashville, Tennessee. 17 March
1994.

"Tickling the Student's Ear: Collaboration and the Teacher/Student
Relationship." (With Anne Welsh). *The Association of English Graduate
Students Conference.* West Coast University, Los Angeles. 12 March
1994.

"Looking for and Pointing to the Meaning: Gazes, Gestures, and Semantics
in the Abortion Question Segment of the Vice-Presidential Debate."
The Language of the Vice-Presidential Debate Symposium. West Coast
University, Los Angeles. 11 December 1992.

"The Business of Marriage in Behn's *Lucky Chance.*" *The Western Society for
Eighteenth-Century Studies Conference.* CSU, San Marcos, California. 15
February 1992.

"Empowering the Student Writer." *The Pacific Southwest Women's Studies
Association Conference.* UC, Irvine, California. 6 April 1991.

"Empowering the Writer: A Response to the Placement of the 18th
Century Voice and the Potential for the Student Voice." *The International
Rhetoric Council Conference.* USD, San Diego. 17 November 1990.

"The Limits of Language in the 18th Century Novel." *The Restoration
and 18th Century Women's Voices Conference.* USD, San Diego. 9
February 1990.

PROFESSIONAL MEMBERSHIPS:

Conference on College Composition and Communication
Modern Language Association

REFERENCES:

Professor James A. Ross, English/Rhetoric (West Coast University)
Professor Michael Green, English (West Coast University)
Professor Eric Gustaf, English (West Coast University)
Professor Susan Richlin (West Coast University)

Sample Economics Vita for a Tenure-Track Position at a Research/Teaching University

On-Line: http://www.hss.caltech.edu/~jwpatty/jobcand/index.html
There you will find various universities listed. Click on UCLA, for example.
You will see a list of candidates on the market. Click on one and see his or her
c.v. If you look at ten or so, you will realize they are very similar and you will
see the information that new candidates convey to employers.

Sample Science Cover Letter for a Tenure-Track Position at a Research/Teaching University

October 20, 1993   160 West Avenue, Apt. G
                                                    New Orleans, Louisiana 70115

Professor Gary Anderson
Department of Chemistry
West Coast University
P. O. Box 200
West Coast, California 92101

Dear Professor Anderson:

I am writing in regard to the professor of chemistry position which
was advertised in *Chemical & Engineering* News in the Oct. 4 issue.
Having earned my Ph.D. in July, 1993, I am currently teaching at
Southern University as a visiting assistant professor. I would like to

continue my career in academia, and I believe my enthusiasm toward teaching and my planned research in antibiotic production by microorganisms would fit in well at West Coast University.

As indicated on the enclosed resumé, I received my B.S. in biochemistry from East Coast Tech in 1988, and went on to study natural products chemistry at the University of the Sea. Though my Ph.D. is from an oceanographic department, and I am qualified to teach basic oceanography courses, my thesis work was concentrated on separation science and structure elucidation of biologically-active compounds. I have worked primarily on the organic chemistry of microorganisms, investigating antibiosis in marine environments. In this process, I isolated and cultured over 600 strains of bacteria and fungi, then extracted, separated and identified the active compounds from the cultures. In addition, I maintained a 200 MHz NMR facility for more than three years and trained our group on the use of a new Varian 500 MHz NMR.

I am very committed to teaching as well as learning. During this academic year, I am teaching a large undergraduate organic chemistry course and a graduate level organic spectroscopy course. This valuable experience has been both challenging and rewarding.

In the future, I would like continue to teach chemistry at a liberal arts university which is focussed on undergraduate education. I would also like to combine all of my organic, biochemical, and microbiological background to develop a research program focussed on the structure elucidation of biologically active compounds from marine bacteria. This program would be particularly well suited to undergraduate research.

I think my diverse experience and my enthusiasm would be valuable to your university. Enclosed are copies of my transcripts, resumé, teaching philosophy, and research plans. If you would like any further information, please contact me at (504) 865-2211 (work) or (504) 897-5257 (home).

Sincerely,

Dr. Brooke Westin

enclosures

Sample Science vita for a Tenure-Track Position at a Research/Teaching University

---

BROOKE A. WESTIN
160 West Avenue, Apt. G
New Orleans, Louisiana 70115
Ph: (504) 865-2211

Professional Objective

To be a professor of chemistry in a teaching-based institution with responsibilities which include teaching core curriculum classes in chemistry, advanced organic chemistry, and spectroscopy and carrying out basic research in the area of microbial organic chemistry.

Education

University of the Sea		*West City, CA*
Ph.D.	Chemistry	1993

East Coast Tech		*East Coast, VA*
B.S.	Biochemistry	1988

Work Experience

Southern University   *New Orleans, LA*

7/93–present   VISITING ASSISTANT PROFESSOR OF CHEMISTRY. Current responsibilities include designing and teaching a large undergraduate organic chemistry section and a graduate organic spectroscopy course with emphasis on NMR techniques.

University of the Sea   *West City, CA*

10/89–6/93   SEA GRANT TRAINEE. Investigated antibiosis in microbial isolates from an estuary in Southern California and a mangrove in Belize. Purified and identified many known antibiotics and several novel antibiotic and anti-inflammatory compounds. Maintained a Bruker 200MHz NMR, and trained research group on the use of a new Varian 500 MHz NMR.

10/88–10/89   RESEARCH ASSISTANT. Learned advanced spectroscopic and separation techniques needed to purify and identify natural products. Isolated several potent neurotoxins from gorgonians. Made semi-synthetic analogs to study the structure-activity relationship between the toxins and the acetylcholine receptor.

Chemical Company, Inc.

3/87–9/87   CO-OP BIOCHEMIST. Designed and executed experimental protocols in fermentation pilot facility for optimization of recombinant E. coli processes. Developed computer program to track recombinant protein through fermentation and purification process steps.

Chemical Company, Inc.

12/85–3/86   CO-OP CHEMICAL ENGINEER. Designed and implemented use of a computerized logsheet for Telomer B Alcohol. Managed quality control program for the Fluorochemicals Group.

6/85–9/85   CO-OP CHEMICAL ENGINEER. Planned and supervised the installation of a computer monitor on Diamines process. Worked with various in-house software as well as VAX electronic messaging software systems.

Honors   American Institute of Chemists Outstanding Senior Award, 1988

T. Marshall Hahn Engineering Scholarship, 1983

Phi Kappa Phi Honor Society, 1986-1988

Gamma Beta Phi Honor Society, 1983-1988

Activities   American Chemical Society, 1990-present

Alpha Chi Sigma Professional Chemistry Fraternity, 1986–present

Alpha Chi Sigma, Gamma Iota chapter vice-president, 1988

East Coast Tech Varsity Volley Ball Team, 1983–87, MVP 1983

Society of Women Engineers, 1983–86

Read and write French. Interests include golf, guitar, camping, SCUBA diving, bicycling, and wildlife rehabilitation.

Publications

Abrams, N. N., Westin, B. A., Toole, D. M., Henry, E. E., Fend, W., & P. Thomas. "Structure/ Activity and Molecular Modeling Studies of the Lophotoxin Family of Irreversible Nicotinic Receptor Antagonists." JOURNAL OF CHEMICAL MEDICINE, 1991, 13, 200–240.

Johnson, B. J., & J. A. Punch (Westin). "Some Primary and Secondary Metabolites of Hypersaline Microbial Mats and Associated Sediments." GENERAL & APPLIED ASPECTS OF HALOPHILIC MICROORGANISMS. edited by M. Mendoza, Pluto Press, Virginia, 1991.

Fend, W., Jons, P. R., Gregory, K., Puttman, C., Westin, B. A., D. Thomas. "Anti-tumor Antibiotics from Marine Microorganisms" from TROISIÈME SYMPOSIUM SUR LES SUBSTANCES NATURELLES D'INTÉRÊT BIOLOGIQUE DE LA RÉGION PACIFIQUE-ASIE. edited by D. Cebit, P. Arnade, D. Lauren, & J. Cosgray Nouméa, Nouvelle-Calédonie, 26–30 Août, 1991.

Westin, B. A., Thomas, D. M., Jons, P. R., Driver, R., Fend, W., McKnight, T., Irish, C., Strong, T. J., & J. Claris. "Salinamides A and

B: Anti-inflammatory Depsipeptides from a Marine Streptomycete." JOURNAL OF THE CHEMICAL SOCIETY. submitted.

Westin, B. A., Jons, P. R., & W. Fend. "Guaymasols: Novel Bacterial Metabolites from a Deep-Ocean Isolate." in preparation.

Westin, B. A., Jons, P. R., & W. Fend. "Surfactamide: A Novel Analog of Surfactin, Isolated from a Deep-Sea species of *Bacillus*." in preparation.

Westin, J. A., Graves, M., & W. Fend. "Antibiotics from Mangrove Isolates: Isolation of *cis*-Cascarillic Acid from a Marine Bacterium." in preparation.

Westin, B. A. "A Chemical Study of Microbial Antibiosis in Estuarine and Extreme Marine Environments." Ph.D. Thesis. University of the Sea. 1993.

References

Dr. William H. Fend (Research Advisor)
University of the Sea
Marine Research Division, 021
West City, California 92101
(619)532-2213

Dr. D. John Find (Curricular Advisor)
University of the Sea
Marine Research Division, 021
West City, California 92101
(619)532-4255

Dr. William All (Professor, Southern University)
Chemistry Department
201 Chemistry Hall
Southern University
New Orleans, Louisiana 70115

TEACHING INTERESTS

My teaching interests include the chemistry core curriculum, advanced organic chemistry, and several advanced chemistry elective courses. These electives include: 1) natural products chemistry, focussing on useful compounds, such as drugs and dyes, which were originally isolated from plants or animals; and 2) organic spectroscopy, including mass spectrometry, infrared, ultraviolet, and especially nuclear magnetic resonance spectroscopy as tools in the identification of organic compounds.

RESEARCH PLANS

Since the discovery of penicillin in 1929, an enormous amount of research investment has gone into the discovery of clinically-useful natural products from microorganisms. Greater than 10,000 bio-active agents have been isolated from microbial sources, with over 5000 antibiotic compounds coming from terrestrial bacteria in a single taxonomic group, the order Actinomycetales. The rate of discovering novel products from this group has been declining steadily in recent decades, requiring investigation of new sources of microbial products. Marine microorganisms provide such a resource. Marine environments can be subject to extreme salinity, temperature, and pressure ranges, effecting physiological adaptations which are not found in terrestrial environments. This has resulted in great taxonomic diversity among marine microorganisms.

As a new source of microbial natural products, marine bacteria have only begun to be examined. My thesis work was dedicated to the chemical investigation of antibiotics produced by such microorganisms, primarily isolates from estuarine environments. I would like to continue with similar work, investigating the organic chemistry of microorganisms from different marine environments, focussing on biologically active natural products. This interdisciplinary work requires the strong background in organic chemistry which I have developed at the University of the Sea. Isolation of natural products will rely heavily on silica and size-exclusion chromatography and especially high-performance liquid chromatography (HPLC). Identification of these compounds will be based primarily on modern nuclear magnetic resonance (NMR) experiments, as well as on infrared and ultraviolet spectroscopy and mass spectrometry.

Realizing that West Coast University expects excellence in teaching as well as research, I would like to design a research program which emphasizes scientific method and applied chemical techniques.

As research in organic chemistry continues to evolve, it will incorporate more collaborative efforts with the biological sciences, as it has in bio-organic chemistry and, more recently, in synthetic organic chemistry. Toward this end, I believe students will benefit from my research approach, offering a solid background in chemical methodology applied to biological systems.

I would be happy to provide a more detailed account of my proposed research or to present a seminar on my thesis research.

TEACHING PHILOSOPHY

Chemistry is a field that progresses rapidly, causing an immense amount of information to be considered fundamental. Thus, an efficient teaching strategy is needed to make the subject less intimidating to the student and professor alike. I believe there are five important elements to this strategy, the most crucial to a university being faculty education.

Teaching modern chemical principles requires continual exposure to current and detailed research as well as exposure to different fields of chemistry. It is difficult for chemistry faculty to get this exposure. I would address this need by organizing a series of seminars for faculty members and senior students. Lecturers would be drawn from government, industry, and academic research environments, to speak on one general topic in organic chemistry per semester.

The second element, curriculum, is the most basic responsibility of a professor. It requires frequent revision and constant analysis. Textbook selection and reference material should reflect the direction of the course. A general chemistry class should provide a link to a student's professional goals or personal life, using human biochemical examples for pre-med students, or even cooking examples for non-science majors. In contrast, an advanced class should develop professional competence in using references and in continuing to learn chemistry without the aid of the instructor. In addition to textbooks, advanced courses should include sections on the exciting areas in modern chemistry, such as environmental chemistry, biotechnology, "stealth" polymers, and fullerenes.

Lectures should involve much more than the curriculum; they should stimulate students through creative presentation of the material. Today's students have grown up using computers, and they are comfortable with very complex software packages. There are many concepts, e.g. *cis* and *trans* isomers, which could be presented well with computer models. Models kits are also invaluable in teaching students to visualize molecules. Many other useful visual aids are available, such as the film documentaries of chemistry fundamentals by R. Hoffman, "Our World of Chemistry." My goal is to integrate all of these teaching materials into a more exciting chemistry class.

Personalized instruction is also needed to develop logical thought processes in beginning students and to instigate original thought in advanced students. This communication can be developed through laboratory instruction or by requiring several office visits per semester by each student. Where possible, I think it is important to convert student laboratories to microscale, also. This provides a safer environment for the student, cuts costs on waste disposal, and more closely reflects the typical skills required in modern industrial positions.

The final element to my teaching strategy is undergraduate research. Students must be encouraged to achieve in organic chemistry to give them confidence that they can apply what they have learned. As my future research proposal indicates, I would like to conduct basic research in bio-organic chemistry which would allow students to design their own experimental protocols and become competent with many of the tools they will be using in their careers.

By following these strategies, I believe I can improve the average student's view of chemistry and excite chemistry majors. I will strive to keep up with current research in all fields of biochemistry and organic chemistry and to motivate students by presenting class materials in creative and effective ways on both a class and an individual level.

Sample Humanities *Vita* for a Tenure-Track Position at a Community College

P. KEVIN PARKER
Department of English
Taper Hall of Humanities 420 MC-0354

403 W. 7th St. #302
Long Beach, CA 90813

University of Southern California
Los Angeles, CA 90089-0354
(213) 740-2808

(310) 495-0331
kparker@scf.usc.edu

EDUCATION

Ph.D. (In progress)	University of Southern California English: Rhetoric, Linguistics, and Literature
M.A. English	University of Missouri, May 1992 Major Area: Rhetoric and Composition
B.A. Comparative Lit.	University of California, Irvine, March 1990
A.A. and A.S.	Saddleback Community College, June 1983 and 1987

ACADEMIC EXPERIENCE

Instructor	Long Beach City College, Spring 1994–present
Adjunct Faculty	Pepperdine University, Fall 1994 Spring 1995
Instructor	Neighborhood Academic Initiative, 1993–94, University of Southern California. Language Arts Instructor for the Pre-College Enrichment Academy
Assistant Lecturer	Freshman Writing Program, University of Southern California, Fall 1993–present
Consultant	Writing Center, University of Southern California, 1993.
Computer Lab Consultant	Writing Center, University of Southern California, 1993
Teaching Assistant	University of Southern California, 1992–93 Courses assisted: American Literature (short fiction), Freshman Honors Seminar
Graduate Instructor	University of Missouri, 1990–92. Courses taught: Freshman Composition, Computers and Composition.

Research Assistant	University of Missouri, 1991–92. Assisted Chair of English Department with construction of bibliographies for books, journals, and articles.
Tutor	University of Missouri Writing Lab, 1990–92. Assisted students with writing in all disciplines, conducted documentation workshops, presented lab introductions.

PUBLICATIONS

Popular Culture in the Composition Classroom, *The Writing Instructor*, v. 13, n. 3, Spring 1994 (with Dawn Formo)

Obsession, Mastery, and the Discourse of Instruction, *Montana English Journal*, n. 1, 1993

"Discourse and the Structure of Obsession," *Mots-Arts*, Spring 1991

PROFESSIONAL ACTIVITIES

Managing Editor	*The Writing Instructor*, 1995–96
Chair	The CCCC Conventions: Conversations Shaping and Transcending Boundaries, CCCC, March 1996
Instructional	University of Southern California's Freshman Writing Program
Coordinator	Writing Center—Computer Assisted Writing Lab, 1994–1995
Associate Chair	Medieval Religious Rhetoric Panel, CCCC, March 1994
Editorial Board	*The Writing Instructor*, 1993–present
Assistant Editor	*Newsletter of the Freudian Field*, 1991–92
Assistant Coordinator	History and Hysteria Conference, University of Missouri, November 1991
Committee Member	Undergraduate Studies Committee, University of Missouri, 1991–92

CONFERENCE PRESENTATIONS

"Getting Trapped in the Web: A Response to J. Hillis Miller's 'The Ethics of Hypertext,'" 25th Annual Spring Rhetoric Conference, USC, February 1995

"Unloading the Canon: Reading, Writing, and Teaching on the Margins," CCCC, Nashville, March 1994

"Computers, Composition, and Collaborative Writing: A Collaborative Presentation" (with David E. Phillips), CCCC, San Diego, April 1993

"'My Name is Kevin and I'm a Writer:' Borrowing from the Twelve Steps to Effect the Pain of Writing," Far West Popular Culture Conference, Las Vegas, January 1993

"Rhetoric, Reggae, and Surf Culture," 1992 American Culture Association, Louisville, March 1992

"Writing Affect: Towards a More Lacanian Notion of Writing," 1992 Graduate Student Conference, University of Missouri, February 1992

"Wise Tiresias's Judgement: The Hysteric's Question in Christa Wolf's 'Self-Experiment: An Appendix to a Report,'" History and Hysteria Conference, University of Missouri, November 1991

LANGUAGES

French   Reading Knowledge

AWARDS

Departmental Fellowships, Departments of English and Thematic Options, University of Southern California, 1992–93

Graduate Teaching Assistantship, University of Missouri, 1990–92

Mots-Arts Non-Fiction Award, Spring 1991

PROFESSIONAL ORGANIZATIONS

National Council of Teachers of English

Modern Language Association

REFERENCES

W. Ross Winterowd

Bruce R. McElderry Professor

Department of English
University of Southern California
Taper Hall of Humanities 420 MC-0354
Los Angeles, CA 90089-0354
(213) 740-2808

Irene Clark
Writing Center Director
Expository Writing Program
University of Southern California
938 W. 34th Street
HSS 201 MC-0062
Los Angeles, CA 90089-0062

Ronald Gottesman
Department of English
University of Southern California
Taper Hall of Humanities 420 MC-0354
Los Angeles, CA 90089-0354
(213) 740-2808

Gary Nagy
English Department Chair
Long Beach City College
4901 East Carson Street
Long Beach, CA 90808
(310) 420-4358

Sample Cover Letter for a Nonfaculty Position

March 30, 1997

262 South Street, Apt. 524
Los Angeles, CA 90089

Employment Representative
Employment Division120 Snelling Ave.
University Park, MN 55113

Dear Employment Representative:

This is to express my interest in the position of Manager, Libraries Publications/Public Relations (job #02697). I believe that this position is one that I am fully prepared to fill, and that I would bring to the job both expertise and enthusiasm.

In my current position, I work as part of a comprehensive publications and public relations team. We work together to plan our communications strategies and budget needs, and we collaborate on the office's high profile publications. In addition, each of us serves as the primary contact for a number of specific projects, seeing them through from conception and planning to writing, designing, production, and delivery. Thus I feel I have a thorough knowledge of the processes needed to plan and implement a multi-faceted communications strategy.

In past positions, I have supervised staff assistants as well as writing interns. Although my current position does not require formal supervisory duties, I believe that working in an office where the stress levels are often high has taught me much about ways in which good supervisors can maintain morale while inspiring staff to make their best efforts.

I would welcome an opportunity to step into the responsibilities involved in managing publications and public relations for the University Libraries. In addition, I would bring a high degree of enthusiasm to this position. As a student of literature and a researcher, I feel deeply about the importance of the Libraries within the University. Over the past few years, I have watched with appreciation the expansion of the Libraries system—both in terms of physical space here and on other campuses, and in terms of exploring new information technologies. The Libraries would clearly be an exciting organization to join.

I would appreciate the opportunity to discuss this position further. Thank you for your time and attention.

Sincerely,

Amanda Taylor

Sample *Vita* (Resume) for a Non-faculty Position

Amanda Taylor   262 South Street, Apt. 524
                                                        Los Angeles, CA 90089
                                                           (213) 555-1212

EDUCATION

Ph.D. candidate in English, University of Southern California, January
1994–present
All course work and comprehensive exams completed April 1997
Dissertation in progress: "Sisters and Citizens: Women Writing Society in
the Early American Republic"

M.A. in English, University of Southern California, 1993

B.A. in English, with high distinction and honors in writing, University of
San Diego, 1989
Phi Beta Kappa
Henry Sams Award for best undergraduate thesis in English writing
option, 1989
Katey Lehman Award for fiction writing, 1989
University of San Diego Scholars Program, 1985–1989

PROFESSIONAL EXPERIENCE

Writer/Editor, July 1995–present
Undergraduate Admissions Office, University of Southern California
• write, edit, proofread, and manage production for various admissions
  publications
• assist in assessing and planning communication strategies
• assist in development of admissions web site
• design Powerpoint slideshows for use in presentations to students and
  parents
• present information to prospective students and parents in group
  information sessions, one-on-one interviews, and by phone

Acting Graduate School Editor, 1993-1995
and *Assistant Thesis Editor,* 1991-1992
Thesis Office, Graduate School, University of Southern California

- copyedited, proofread, and managed production for a variety of publications
- copyedited theses and dissertations in all disciplines
- supervised one staff assistant

Writer/Editor, 1989–1991
Institute for the Study of Adult Literacy, University of Southern California
- wrote, edited, proofread, and provided desktop publishing for a wide variety of documents
- developed press releases and coordinated publicity efforts with College of Education and Public Information staff
- assisted grant writers with research and writing of grant proposals
- served as managing editor for a 5,000-circulation research newsletter
- supervised student interns

ACADEMIC PUBLICATIONS

Assistant Editor, *American Women Fiction Writers to 1820* for Dictionary of Literary Biography series. Ed. Susana Smith with Amanda Taylor. Bruccoli-Clark-Layman. Scheduled for publication 2000 [in press].

"Susan B. Anthony" (co-authored with Ann Hein) and "Charolette Perkins Gilman" in *American Women Fiction Writers to 1820* [in press].

"Edith Wharton" in *Encyclopedia of American Women's Literature.* Ed. Charles Van Vechten. New York: Continuum [in press].

"Benedict Anderson" and "Gordon Wood" in *Historians and Historical Writing.* Ed. Kelly Fitzpatrick. Fitzroy Dearborn: London and Chicago [in press].

"American Historical and Political Prose," "Literature and Politics," "Edith Wharton," and "Theodore Roethke," in *United State's Guide to Literature in English.* Ed. Mark Bauer. Fitzroy Dearborn: London and Chicago, 1996.

COMPUTER SKILLS

Desktop publishing using Pagemaker
Powerpoint presentation development
Web page development (see my personal page at
   http://www.personal.xxxxx/)
Familiarity with both PC and Mac operating environments,
   ISIS student information system

OTHER PROFESSIONAL DEVELOPMENT

Member, Toastmasters International (public speaking organization)

University of Southern California Human Resources Professional Development Courses (transcript of courses available upon rerquest)

SERVICE

Writing Consultant, University of Southern California Summer Research Opportunity Program, 1994–1997

Writing Workshop for Expository Writing Program students, 1993, 1995, 1996

Portfolio of publications, complete academic vita, *and references are available on request.*

Suggested Reading and Resource List

Academic Mysteries

Here are some mystery titles suggested and annotated by our innovative contributor Casie Hermansson. Since these fictional works deal with the very human
side of academic job searches, they can help you understand some of the everyday realities behind those mystical hiring decisions that can seem so perplexing.

We hope that you will also use them to imagine search committee members as complex human beings rather than stick-figure gatekeepers who
must be placated with ritualistic interview responses. Most important, read
them because you need a little fun in your job search.

Borthwick, J. S. *The Student Body*. NY: St. Martin's P, 1986.
From the perspective of new faculty.
Cross, Amanda. (a.k.a. Carolyn Heilbrun, academic).
Anything in her academic mystery series.
Jones, D.J.H. *Murder at the MLA*. Athens: U Georgia P, 1993.
Revolves around a hiring committee in action.
Kenney, Susan. *Graves in Academe*. NY: Viking, 1985.
From the perspective of new faculty.

Kramer, John E., Jr. and John E. Kramer III. *College Mystery Novels: An Annotated Bibliography, Including a Guide to Professorial Series-Character Sleuths.* NY and London: Garland, 1983.
The guide Hermansson uses to locate mysteries.

Neel, Janet. *Death Among the Dons.* NY: St. Martin's, 1993.
Narrative perspective with the faculty set in women's college (UK). Depicts lots of committee meetings.

Raphael, Lev. *Let's Get Criminal: An Academic Mystery.* NY: St. Martin's, 1996
———. *The Edith Wharton Murders: A Nick Hoffman Mystery* . NY: St. Martin's P, 1997.
Both of these are written from the perspective of Nick Hoffman, a lecturer in English, whose partner is the creative writer on faculty.

Wender, Theodora. *Knight Must Fall.* NY: Avon, 1985.
Revolves around a search on campus.

Business Interviewing Guides

Since the majority of these business self-help titles are available in university and public libraries, you can consult them without investing large amounts of money. Your real task here is to wrest them out of the hands of the undergraduates during key clinches in the job search cycle.

Allen, Jeffrey G. *The Complete Q & A Job Interview Book.* NY: Wiley, 1988.
———. *Jeff Allen's Best: Get the Interview.* NY: Wiley, 1990.
———. *Jeff Allen's Best: Win the Job.* NY: Wiley, 1990.
———. *The Perfect Follow-Up Method to Get the Job.* NY: Wiley, 1992.
Ball, Frederick W. *Killer Interviews.* NY: McGraw-Hill, 1996.
Beatty, Richard H. *The Five Minute Interview.* NY: Wiley, 1986.
———. *175 High-Impact Cover Letters.* NY: Wiley , 1996.
———. *The New Complete Job Search.* NY: Wiley, 1992.
———. *The Resume Kit.* 2nd edition. NY: Wiley, 1991.
———. *International Careers.* Holbrook, MA: B. Adams, 1990.
Baridon, Andrea P. and David R. Eyler. *Working Together: New Rules and Realities for Managing Men and Women at Work.* NY: McGraw-Hill, 1994.
Bell, Arthur H. *The Complete Manager's Guide to Interviewing: How to Hire the Best.* Homewood, IL: Dow Jones-Irwin, 1989.

———. *Extraviewing: Innovative Ways to Hire the Best*. Homewood, IL: Business One, 1992.

Berman, Jeffrey A. *Competence-Based Employment Interviewing*. Westport, Conn: Quorum, 1997.

Black, James Menzies. *How to Get Results from Interviewing, A Practical Guide for Operating Management*. Malabar, FL: R.E. Krieger Publishing Co., 1982.

Boldt, Laurence G. *Zen and the Art of Making a Living: A Practical Guide to Creative Career Design*. NY: Morrow, 1992.

Booher, Dianna. *Communicate with Confidence!* NY: McGraw-Hill, 1994.

Bostwick, Burdette E. *111 Proven Techniques and Strategies for Getting the Job Interview*. NY: Wiley, 1981.

———. *Resume Writing: A Comprehensive How-to-Do-It Guide*. NY: Wiley, 1990.

Breakwell, Glynis M. *Coping with Threatened Identities*. NY: Methuen, 1986.

———. *Interviewing*. NY: Routledge, 1990.

Corwen, Leonard. *Successful Job Hunting*. Charleston, WV: Cambridge Educational, 1995.

———. *Your Resume: Key to a Better Job*. NY: Arco, 1988.

Curzon, Susan Carol. *Managing the Interview, a How-to-Do-It Manual for Hiring Staff*. NY: Neal Schuman Publishers, 1995.

DeLuca, Matthew J. *Best Answers to the 201 Most Frequently Asked Interview Questions*. NY: McGraw-Hill, 1997.

Drake, John D. *The Perfect Interview: How to Get the Job You Really Want*. 2nd ed. NY: AMACOM, 1997.

———. *The Effective Interviewer: A Guide for Managers*. NY: American Management Association, 1989.

Eder, Robert W. and Gerald R. Ferris, eds. *The Employment Interview: Theory, Research, and Practice*. Newbury Park: Sage Publications, 1989.

Eyler, David R. *Job Interviews that Mean Business*. NY: Random House, 1992.

———. *Resumes that Mean Business*. NY: Random House, 1996.

Falcone, Paul. *96 Great Interview Questions to Ask Before You Hire*. NY: AMACOM, 1997.

French, Albert L. *How to Locate Jobs and Land Interviews, A Complete Guide, Reference and Resource Book for the Job Hunter*. Denver, CO: High Pine Publications, 1991.

Fry, Ronald. *101 Great Answers to the Toughest Interview Questions*. 3rd edition. Franklin Lakes, NJ: Career Press, 1996.

———. *Work Evaluation and Adjustment: An Annotated Bibliograhy*. Menomonie, WI: Materials Development Center, School of Education and Human Services. U of Wisconsin-Stout, 1986.

Goodale, James G. *The Fine Art of Interviewing*. Englewood Cliffs, NJ: Prentice-Hall, 1982.

———. *One to One, Interviewing, Selecting, Appraising, and Counseling Employees*. Englewood Cliffs, NJ: Prentice Hall, 1992.

Heiberger, Mary Morris and Julia Miller Vick. *The Academic Job Search Handbook*. 2nd ed. Philadelphia, U of Pennsylvania P, 1996.

Hickman, Linda and Cliff Longman. *Business Interviewing*. Reading, MA: Addison-Wesley, 1994.

Johnson, William Courtney. *The Career Match Method: Getting the Job You Want in the '90s*. NY: Wiley, 1992.

Jud, Brian. *Job Search 101*. Avon, CT: Marketing Directions, 1991

Kanter, Arnold B. *The Essential Book of Interviewing, Everything You Need to Know from Both Sides of the Table*. NY: Times Books, 1995.

King, Julie Adair. *The Smart Woman's Guide to Interviewing and Salary Negotiation*. 2nd ed. Franklin Lakes, NJ: Career Press, 1995.

Kohlmann, James D. *Make Them Choose You: The Executive Selection Process, Replacing Mystery with Strategy*. Englewood Cliffs, NJ: Prentice Hall, 1988.

Krannich, Caryl Rae. *Dynamite Answers to Interview Questions, No More Sweaty Palms!* Woodbridge, VA: Impact Publications, 1992.

———. *Interview for Success*. 3rd ed. Manassas, VA: Impact Publications, 1990.

Krannich, Ronald L. and Caryl Raie Krannich. *Complete Guide to International Jobs and Careers*. Manassas Park, VA: Impact Publicatons, 1992.

———. *The Complete Guide to Public Employment*. Woodridge, VA: Impact Publications, 1990.

———. *Discover the Right Job for You*. Woodbridge, VA: Impact Publications, 1991.

Kuman, Arthur, Jr. and Richard D. Salmon. *The Job Hunter's Guide to 100 Great American Cities, A National Employment Directory*. Latham, NY: Brattle Communications, 1991.

Medley, H. Anthony. *Sweaty Palms: The Neglected Art of Being Interviewed*. Berkeley, CA: Ten Speed Press, 1992.

Marcus, John. *The Complete Job Interview Handbook*. 2nd ed. NY: Barnes and Noble Books, 1988.

Merman, Stephen K., and John E. McLaughlin. *Out-Interviewing the Interviewer: A Job Winner's Script for Success*. Englewood Cliffs, NJ: Prentice-Hall, 1983.

Messmer, Max. *50 Ways to Get Hired*. NY: William Morrow and Co., Inc., 1994.

Pinsker, Richard J. *Hiring Winners: Profile, Interview, Evaluate*. NY: AMACOM, 1991.

Rafe, Stephen C. *Get Hired--It's Your Job*. NY: Harper Business, 1990.

Skopec, Eric W. *Situational Interviewing*. NY: Harper and Row, 1986.

Stoodley, Martha. *Information Interviewing, What It Is and How to Use It in Your Career*. Garrett Park, MD: Garrett Park P, 1990.

Tieger, Paul D. and Barbara Barron-Tieger. *Do What You Are*. Boston: Little, Brown & Co., 1992.

Uris, Auren. *88 Mistakes Interviewers Make—and How to Avoid Them*. NY: American Management Association, 1988.

——— and John J. Tarrant. *Career Stages: Surmounting the Crises of Working Life*. NY: Seaview/Putnam, 1983.

Wilson, Susan B. *Your Intelligent Heart: Notes to Women Who Work*. NY: AMACOM, 1995.

Wise, Jacquie. *Career Comeback: Taking Charge of Your Career*. Melbourne: Pitman, 1991.

Yeager, Neil M. and Lee Hough. *Power Interviews, Job Winning Tactics from Fortune 500 Recruiters*. NY: Wiley, 1990.

———. *CareerMap: Deciding What you Want, Getting It, and Keeping It*. NY: Wiley, 1988.

Leonard Bernstein Videos

Bernstein models the passionate teacher/performer in these videos from the "Young People's Concerts" series. There are up to three episodes on each videocassette.

(1) *Humor in Music*; (2) *What Is a Melody?* Dir. Leonard Bernstein. Leonard Bernstein's Young People's Concerts with the New York Philharmonic,

New York: Sony Classical, videocassette, 1993.

(1) *Jazz in the Concert Hall*; (2) *A Tribute to Sibelius*; (3) *A Birthday Tribute to Shostakovich*. Dir. Leonard Bernstein. Leonard Bernstein's Young People's Concerts with the New York Philharmonic, New York: Sony Classical, videocassette, 1993.

(1) *What Does Music Mean?*; (2) *What Is Orchestration?* Dir. Leonard Bernstein. Leonard Bernstein's Young People's Concerts with the New York Philharmonic, New York: Sony Classical, videocassette, 1993.

(1) *Musical Atoms: A Study of Intervals*; (2) *Quiz Concert: How Musical Are You?* Dir. Leonard Bernstein. Leonard Bernstein's Young People's Concerts with the New York Philharmonic, New York: Sony Classical, videocassette,1993.

(1) *Berlioz Takes a Trip*; (2) *Two Ballet Birds; Fidelio*; (3) *A Celebration of the Life*. Dir. Leonard Bernstein. Leonard Bernstein's Young People's Concerts with the New York Philharmonic, New York: Sony Classical, videocassette, 1993.

(1) *What Is a Concert?* (2) *What Is American Music?* Dir. Leonard Bernstein. Leonard Bernstein's Young People's Concerts with the New York Philharmonic, New York: Sony Classical, videocassette, 1993. 1 video-cassette (118 min): sd, black and white, mono, 1/2 in.

Psychology of the Job Search

These offerings directly or implicitly approach the elements of human interaction in the job search, most of them from an overtly scholarly stance.

Axtell, Roger E. *Gestures, the Do's and Taboos of Body Language Around the World*. NY: Wiley, 1991.

Beebe, Steven A. and Susan J. Beebe. *Interpersonal Communication: Relating to Others*. Boston: Allyn and Bacon, 1996.

Breakwell, Glynis M. and David V. Canter, eds. *Empirical Approaches to Social Representations*. NY: Oxford UP, 1993.

Chirban, John T. *Interviewing in Depth: The Interactive-Relational Approach*. Thousand Oaks, CA: Sage Publications, 1996.

Cook, Mark, ed. *Issues in Person Perception*. NY: Methuen, 1984.

Douglas, Jack D. *Creative Interviewing*. Beverly Hills: Sage Publications, 1985.

Elgin, Suzette Haden. *Try to Feel It My Way: New Help for Touch Dominant*

People and Those Who Care About Them. NY: Wiley, 1997.

———. *BusinessSpeak: Using the Gentle Art of Verbal Persuasion to Get What You Want at Work.* NY: McGraw-Hill, 1995.

———. *Genderspeak: Men, Women, and the Gentle Art of Verbal Self-Defense.* NY: John Wiley and Sons, Inc., 1993.

Farnell, Brenda, ed. *Human Action Signs in Cultural Context: The Visible and the Invisible in Movement and Dance.* Metuchen, NJ: Scarecrow P, 1995.

Feldman, Robert S., *Applications of Nonverbal Behavioral Theories and Research.* Hillsdale, NJ: Lawrence Earlbaum Associates, 1992.

——— and Bernard Rime. *Fundamentals of Nonverbal Behavior.* NY: Cambridge UP, 1991.

Furnham, Adrian. *Personality at Work: The Role of Individual Differences in the Workplace.* NY: Routledge, 1992.

——— and Michael Argyle, *The Psychology of Social Situations: Selected Readings.* NY: Pergamon P, 1981.

——— and Stephen Bochner, *Culture Shock: Psychological Reactions to Unfamiliar Environments.* NY: Methuen, 1986.

Hargrave, Jan Latiolais. *Let Me See Your Body Talk.* Dubuque, IA: Kendal-Hunt Publishing Co., 1995.

Hargie, Owen D. W., ed. *The Handbook of Communication Skills.* NY: Routledge, 1997.

Higbee, Kenneth L. *Your Memory: How It Works and How to Improve It.* 2nd edition. NY: Marlowe and Company, 1996.

Holstein, James A. and Jaber F. Gubrium. *The Active Interview.* Thousand Oaks, CA: Sage Publications, 1995.

Jennerich, Elaine Z., and Edward J. Jennerich. *The Reference Interview as a Creative Art.* 2nd ed. Englewood, CO: Libraries Unlimited, 1997.

Jones, Stanley. *The Right Touch: Understanding and Using the Language of Physical Contact.* Cresskill, NJ: Hampton P; Annandale, VA: Speech Communication Association, 1994.

Josipovici, Gabriel. *Touch.* New Haven, CT: Yale UP, 1996.

Komter, Martha. *Conflict and Cooperation in Job Interviews: A Study of Talk, Tasks, and Ideas.* Amsterdam, Philadelphia: John Benjamins Pub. Co., 1991.

MacHovec, Frank J. *Interview and Interrogation, A Scientific Approach.* Springfield, IL: C.C. Thomas, 1989.

Marsh, Peter. *Eye to Eye: How People Interact.* Topsfield, Mass: Salem House, 1988.

————. *Eye to Eye: Your Relationships and How They Work*. London: Sidgwick and Jackson, 1988.

Mayo, Clara and Nancy M. Henley. *Gender and Nonverbal Behavior*. NY: Springer-Verlag, 1981.

Minninger, Joan. *Total Recall: How to Boost Your Memory Power*. Emmaus, PA: Rodale P, 1984.

Nathan, Harriet. *Critical Choices in Interviews: Conduct, Use, and Research Role*. Berkeley: Institute of Governmental Studies, U of CA, 1986.

Nicholson, Nigel, ed. *Work and Personality*. Applied Psychology Series. Hove, UK: Psychology P, 1996.

Pedersen, Paul and Allen Ivey. *Culture-Centered Counseling and Interviewing Skills, A Practical Guide*. Westport, CT: Praeger, 1993.

Poyatos, Fernando, ed. *Advances in Nonverbal Communication: Sociocultural, Clinical, Esthetic, and Literary Perspectives*. Philadelphia: John Benjamins Pub. Co., 1992.

————. *Paralanguage: A Linguistic and Interdisciplinary Approach to Interactive Speech and Sound*. Philadelphia: John Benjamin Pub. Co., 1993.

————. *Cross-cultural Perspective in Nonverbal Communication*. NY: Hogrefe 1988

Richmond, Virginia P., James C. McCroskey, and Steven K. Payne. *Nonverbal Behavior in Interpersonal Relations*. 3rd ed. Allyn and Bacon, 1995.

Russell, James A. and Jose Miguel Fernandez-Dols. *The Psychology of Facial Expression*. N. Cambridge UP, 1997.

Ruthrof, Horst. *Semantics and the Body: Meaning from Frege to the Postmodern*. Buffalo: U of Toronto P, 1997.

Segerstrale, Ullica and Peter Molnar, eds. *Nonverbal Communication: Where Nature Meets Culture*. Mahway, NJ: Lawrence Erlbaum Associates, 1997.

Sincoff, Machael Z. and Robert S. Goyer. *Interviewing*. NY: Macmillian, 1984.

Spitz, Herman H. *Nonconscious Movements: From Mystical Messages to Facilitated Communication*. Mahway, NJ: Lawrence Erlbaum and Associates, 1997.

Staw, Barry M., ed. *Psychological Dimensions of Organizational Behavior*. Englewood Cliffs, NJ: Prentice Hall, 1991.

Stewart, Charles J. and William B. Cash, Jr. *Interviewing, Principles and Practices*. 5th ed. Dubuque, IA: W.C. Brown, 1991.

Svenson, Ola, and A. John Maule, eds. *Time Pressure and Stress in Human Judgment and Decision Making.* NY: Plenum P, 1993.

Ting-Toomey, Stella, ed. *The Challenge of Facework, Cross-Cultural and Interpersonal Issues.* Albany: SUNY P, 1994.

Tolor, Alexander, ed. *Effective Interviewing.* Springfield, IL: C. C. Thomas, 1985.

Von Raffler-Engel, Walburga. *The Percepton Of Non-Verbal Behavior in the Career Interview.* Philadelphia: J. Benjamins Publishing Co., 1983.

Feminist Topics

Although these titles directly address women, they contain valuable strategies for both genders.

Aisenberg, Nadya and Mona Harrington. *Women of Academe: Outsiders in the Sacred Grove.* Amherst: U of Massachusetts P, 1988.

Barnett, Rosalind C. *Home-to-Work Spillover Revisited: A Study of Full-Time Employed Women in Dual-Earner Couples.* Wellesley, MA: Center for Research on Women, Wellesley College, 1994.

————, Aline Sayer, and Nancy L. Marshall. *Gender, Job Rewards, Job Concerns and Psychological Distress: A Study of Dual-Earner Couples.* Wellesley, MA: Center for Research on Women, Wellesley College, 1994.

Cameron, Deborah, ed. *The Feminist Critique of Language: A Reader.* New York: Routledge, 1990.

Caplan, Paula J. *Lifting a Ton of Feathers: A Woman's Guide for Surviving in the Academic World.* Buffalo: U of Toronto P, 1993.

Cyr, Dianne and Blaize Horner Reich, eds. *Scaling the Ivory Tower: Stories From Women in Business School Faculties.* Westport, CT: Praeger, 1996.

Lakoff, George. *Women, Fire, and Dangerous Things, What Categories Reveal about the Mind.* Chicago: U of Chicago P, 1987.

Lakoff, George and Mark Johnson. *Metaphors We Live By.* Chicago: U of Chicago P, 1980.

Sandler, Bernice Resnick, Lisa A. Silverberg, and Roberta M. Hall. *The Chilly Classroom Climate: A Guide to Improve the Education of Women.*

Washington, D.C.: National Association for Women in Education, 1996.

Thompson, Irene, ed. *The Road Retaken: Women Reenter the Academy.* NY: MLA, 1985.

Toth, Emily. *Ms. Mentor's Impeccable Advice for Women in Academia.* Philadelphia: U of Pennsylvania P, 1997.

Allen, Jeffrey. *The Complete Question and Answer Job Interview Book*. NY: Wiley, 1988.

Bauer, Dale. *Feminist Dialogics: A Theory of Failed Community*. NY: State U of NY P, 1988.

Burke, Kenneth. *A Rhetoric of Motives*. NY: Prentice-Hall, 1950.

Elgin, Suzette Haden. *BusinessSpeak: Using the Gentle Art of Verbal Persuasion to Get What You Want at Work*. NY: McGraw-Hill, 1995.

————. *Genderspeak: Men, Women, and the Gentle Art of Verbal Self-Defense*. NY: John Wiley & Sons, Inc., 1993.

Holloway, Karla F. C. *Codes of Conduct: Race, Ethics, and the Color of Our Character*. New Jersey: Rutgers UP, 1995.

Hunter, Kathryn Montgomery. *Doctor's Stories: The Narrative Structure of Medical Knowledge*. Princeton, NJ: Princeton UP, 1991.

Jarratt, Susan C. "Feminism and Composition: The Case for Conflict." *Contending with Words: Composition and Rhetoric in a Postmodern Age*. Eds. Patricia Harkin and John Schilb. New York: MLA, 1991. 105–123.

Kalish, Alan. "Learning to Profess: The Enculturation of New Faculty Members in English." Diss. Indiana U, 1997.

Lorde, Audre. "The Master's Tools Will Never Dismantle the Master's

House." *Sister Outsider: Essays and Speechs by Audre Lorde*. Freedom, CA: Crossing, 1984. 110–113.

———. *Sister Outsider: Essays and Speechs by Audre Lorde*. Freedom, CA: Crossing, 1984.

Lunsford, Andrea A. and Cheryl Glenn. "Rhetorical Theory and the Teaching of Writing." *The St. Martin's Guide to Teaching Writing*. Eds. Robert Connors and Cheryl Glenn. NY: St. Martin's P, 1995. 394–407.

Medley, Anthony H. *Sweaty Palms: The Neglected Art of Being Interviewed*. Berkeley, CA: Ten Speed P, 1993.

Phelps, Louise Whetherbee. *Composition as a Human Science: Contributions to the Self-Understanding of a Discipline*. NY: Oxford, UP, 1988.

——— and Janet Emig, eds. *Feminine Principles and Women's Experience in American Composition and Rhetoric*. U of Pittsburgh P, 1995.

Showalter, English, et al. *The MLA Guide to the Job Search: A Handbook for Departments and for Ph.Ds and Ph.D. Candidates in English and Foreign Languages*. NY: MLA, 1996.

Smith, Barbara. "Communicator at the Crossroads: Barbara Smith." *Visionary Voices: Women on Power, Conversations with Shamans, Activists, Teachers, Artists and Healers*. Ed. Penny Rossenwasser. San Francisco: Aunt Lute, 1992. 195–203.

Toth, Emily. *Ms. Mentor's Impeccable Advice for Women in Academia*. Philadelphia: U of Pennsylvania P, 1997.

White, Kate. *Why Good Girls Don't Get Ahead...But Gutsy Girls Do: Nine Secrets Every Career Woman Must Know*. NY: Warner Books, 1995.